"Like many bold women, Sor Juan: as 'ahead of her time.' Theresa Yug in her intelligence, wit, and cando₁ moment and social location, yet she feminist and ecofeminist concerns. anyone interested in Mesoamerican studies in religion, and Catholic feminism."

‗₁₀ı

‗...₁₁ nistory, women's

—SARAH ROBINSON
CLAREMONT GRADUATE UNIVERSITY, CLAREMONT, CA

"Theresa Yugar's imaginative reconstruction of the life of Sor Juana de la Cruz locates the seventeenth-century scholar within the framework of liberation theology and ecofeminism. She demonstrates the ways that communities of women with whom the writer lived influenced Sor Juana's thinking about patriarchy and hierarchy. Further, she shows how natural disasters shaped the nun's views about the environment. Yugar therefore enlarges and expands our understanding of the significance of Sor Juana de la Cruz, taking scholarly considerations of this figure in new directions."

—REBECCA MOORE
SAN DIEGO STATE UNIVERSITY, SAN DIEGO, CA

Sor Juana Inés de la Cruz

Sor Juana Inés de la Cruz

Feminist Reconstruction of Biography and Text

Theresa A. Yugar

Foreword by
Rosemary Radford Ruether

WIPF & STOCK · Eugene, Oregon

SOR JUANA INÉS DE LA CRUZ
Feminist Reconstruction of Biography and Text

Wipf and Stock
An Imprint of Wipf and Stock Publishers
199 W. 8th Ave., Suite 3
Eugene, OR 97401

www.wipfandstock.com

ISBN 13: 978-1-62564-440-4

Manufactured in the U.S.A.   10/22/2014

In loving memory of my mother and father, Jeanne and Juan Raul Yugar, who always encouraged me to follow my *sueños*.

In loving gratitude to Sandy Baldonado, without whom this book would not have been possible; she's the Crone who has earned this Maiden's thanks.

Estudia, arguye y enseña,
y es de la Iglesia servicio,
que no la quiere ignorante
El que racional la hizo.

She studies, and disputes, and teaches,
and thus she serves her Faith;
for how could God, who gave her reason,
want her ignorant?

VILLANCICO, OR, CAROL, IN CELEBRATION
OF ST. CATHERINE OF ALEXANDRIA
SOR JUANA INÉS DE LA CRUZ, 1692

Table of Contents

Illustrations

Foreword

by Dr. Rosemary Radford Ruether

THERESA ANN YUGAR HAS been studying the thought and writings of the seventeenth century Mexican writer, Sor Juana Inés de la Cruz, for more than twenty years. She wrote a Master's thesis on Sor Juana's thought in 1997 at Harvard University and a doctoral thesis at the Claremont Graduate University in 2013. This book on Sor Juana's life and thought is the culmination of her research on this key thinker, but it is undoubtedly not the end of Yugar's work on Sor Juana. She will continue to delve into her writings for the rest of her life. For Yugar, Sor Juana is the foundational figure for Latina feminism and ecofeminism in the Americas. What it means to be fully human as a woman in the context of patriarchal society and church was first explored by Sor Juana in the mid to late seventeenth century in the heartland of the former Mesoamerican empire and its colonial replacement by the Spanish conquerors as Mexico City. The questions she raised then are still relevant today. Latina feminism still looks to Sor Juana as their founding mother and witness, as well as tragic martyr in the struggle for authentic life.

Yugar looks at the shaping of Sor Juana's life and thought in two conflicting contexts. First there is the Mesoamerican world-view that was crushed by the Spanish conquerors but was still very much present in the family and local population in which she grew up, the haciendas of Nepantla and Panoayán outside Mexico City. Second is the world brought to Mexico by the Spaniards that represented their colonial expansion, their championing of the Counter Reformation of the Catholic Church against the

Protestant Reformation and their gender ideology and practices which they developed in Spain and brought to their colonies in the Americas. Sor Juana was not only formed by the interaction of these two cultures, but sees her own vision of redemption as the reconciliation of these two worldviews. Figures representing the Indigenous world of America and the European presence of Spain appear in her writings as two realities that need to come together and be harmonized, rather than the second repressing the first.

Yugar traces the development of Sor Juana's life and culture in three matricentric worlds. First there was the period of her girlhood (1648-61) in which she grew up surrounded by her strong mother, Doña Isabel Ramírez, and her maternal grandmother, Doña Beatriz Rendón, two sisters and two stepsisters. Her father, a Spaniard, was absent and her mother was unmarried, a status Yugar sees as chosen or preferred by her independent mother. Here Sor Juana was part of a world very much run by women as competent administrators of land and haciendas in violation of the Spanish assumption of female subordination to fathers and husbands.

The second stage of Sor Juana's life, from the age of thirteen to twenty (1661-1669) was spent in Mexico City, where she again lived in a female centered context, with two other sisters, a stepsister and her mother's sister, Doña María Ramírez. These women were part of a Creole elite family of Spaniards born in the Americas who had close ties to the vice regal court in the capital city. At sixteen Sor Juana became a lady-in-waiting at the vice regal court and was influenced particularly by the *Vireina* Doña Leonor Carreto. This influential woman was drawn to Juana's intelligence and creativity and nurtured her development as a scholar and writer. Here Juana wrote poems that were read by the elite, sometimes critical of the inequalities she saw around her and the assumptions of women's inferiority. Although such views were not appreciated by the male elite and church leaders, the *Vireina* protected Juana.

As Juana approached her twenties, she was faced with two options for her future. She could marry an elite Spaniard and take her place in the system of male domination of Spanish society or she could enter religious life and become a nun. Convent life appealed to her because it put her into a community of women who were largely in charge of their own institution and resources, and where she would have independence to continue her studies and writings. She first entered a community of Discalced Carmelites which required no dowry, but this community was harsh and she fell ill and left after three months. She went back to the vice regal court where she recovered over the following year. She then was able to secure a dowry to enter the convent of St Paula that gave her better space for own studies and writings. This community also made use of her skills, electing her head-mistress, archivist and treasurer.

In the convent Sor Juana was able to write for both the vice regal court and for the church, composing poems, sonnets, letters and plays for public dissemination. The *virreinas* made her work known in Mexico and also in Spain where they were sent for publication. This was key to the survival of Sor Juana's writings, since by this patronage her work evaded the censorship of the Church and preserved her legacy for the future.

However Sor Juana soon fell into conflict with powerful churchmen who were scandalized by her independent voice. Her confessor, the Jesuit Antonio Núñez de Miranda, had supported her in entering the religious life, but he began to criticize her as a "scandal" for her free production of writings. Consequently Sor Juana relieved him of his position as her confessor. This intensified his criticism of her. This was particularly dangerous for her since he subsequently became head of the tribunal of the Spanish Inquisition in her region.

Sor Juana was also attacked by Manuel Fernández de Santa Cruz, then bishop of Puebla. He published two documents relating to Sor Juana and circulated them throughout Mexico. The first was titled *Carta atenagórica*, or "letter worthy of Athena." Fernández criticized her for differing with the well-known Portuguese Jesuit writer Antonio de Vieyra of Christ's availability to his people. Fernández de Santa Cruz wrote the treatise under a female pseudonym, as Sor Filotea de la Cruz. Sor Juana wrote a treatise named *La Respuesta*, "The Answer," in which she defended her history of writing primarily in secular forms. She maintained also that women were equally intelligent and capable of knowledge. In this treatise she canvases her history of desire for learning from childhood. It is a major source for the biography of Sor Juana.

Sor Juana also wrote another treatise probably a little earlier than *La Respuesta*, called *El Sueño* (The Dream). In this work Sor Juana charts the journey of the "soul" (her soul) through various stages of development, imaged by various mythological figures from the Greek tradition. These two treatises are the only ones written in the first person by Sor Juana who usually writes in the third person. They thus represent writings which are personal and autobiographal. Yugar devotes the second half of her book to a detailed analysis of these two writings. Shortly after finishing the second of these two major writings, Sor Juana acceded to the demands of the church and surrendered her books and scientific instruments to be sold. She devoted herself to the care of the sick and soon after she died. Thus Sor Juana's life ends in what appears to be a martyrdom, in which she appears to accept her own silencing, giving up the creativity that had defined the meaning of life for her since her youth.

In 1974 Sor Juana was acclaimed at a celebration in Mexico City as "the first feminist in the New World." Teresa Yugar speaks of her as an ecofeminist, someone who both sought the equality of women with men, and also the care for and celebration of the beauty of nature. In her times, Sor Juana sought both women's equality in Church and society and care for and harmony with the natural world. She challenged the Church to affirm a fuller vision of what the mission of the church is all about, for both equality and justice for women with men and care for God's creation.

—Rosemary Radford Ruether
Claremont School of Theology and Graduate University

Preface

FOR MORE THAN TWENTY years I have been studying the life and writings of Sor (Sister) Juana Inés de la Cruz, seventeenth-century humanist, philosopher and last great author of *El Siglo de Oro*, Spain's Golden Age of Literature. In 1997, at Harvard Divinity School, I defended my master's thesis on this same woman. Its title was, "The Rise of a Latina Feminist Struggle and Methodology: Exploring the Fruits of Her Heritage, Sor Juana Inés de la Cruz." In it, I examined Sor Juana's God-imagery and Christological perspectives. Her writings suggested that God-imagery transcended gender. God was the center and circumference of all things, Prime Mover, Divine Creator, Great Author, and Merciful Mediator. Sor Juana's Christological perspective was astounding. Inadvertently she compared herself to Jesus, who was also persecuted without a cause in His life. At the time, I asserted that, "Like Christ, called by God to ransom His life for many, Sor Juana also ransomed her life, giving up her books," her lifeline to God and the world.

For my doctoral dissertation I also conducted a feminist historical reconstruction of Sor Juana's life, family background, writings, educational background, life in the vice regal court and convent. However, I vastly expanded the scope of my research. I wanted to do something different from existing Sorjuanista studies. They generally examine various aspects of Sor Juana's vast oeuvre of writings, which includes sixty-five sonnets, sixty-two ballads, thirty-two *loas* (preludes to plays), sixteen sets of *villancicos* (carols for the Church), three *auto sacramentales* (one-act dramas), two comedies, and, "a profusion of *endechas, redondillas, liras, décimas, silvas,* and other metrical forms employed during

Spain's literary Golden Age,"[1] but do not tell her-story in *su propia voz* (her own voice). That is the goal of this book, which grows out of my dissertation project.

Unlike other Sorjuanista scholars, I did not want to repeat the same facts, data and dates that have condensed Sor Juana's life and her-story to Octavio Paz's reductionistic comment that she belonged to a family of strong spirited and enterprising women. Early on, I realized the challenge of this endeavor. A key point is that the majority of Sor Juana's texts about herself were written in the third person. I think there were two reasons why this scholar refrained from speaking in the first person, *en sus propia palabras*, in her own words. First, she was a private person, most likely an introvert. She was a scholar, rather than a mystic, the path normally taken by her European counterparts. Secondly, she was an ordinary Christian woman who lived out her faith with the hope of securing her salvation, with God, upon her death.

This book has two sections. The first section utilizes Elisabeth Schüssler Fiorenza's feminist historical reconstruction methodology as a starting point for an examination of Sor Juana's life from a gender-specific lens. This approach reveals that Sor Juana moved through three communities of women in her lifetime, and is the beginning of a holistic account of Sor Juana's life and texts. The book analyzes all three stages of Sor Juana's life, paying particular attention to her evolving awareness and criticism of inequalities in her region that included sexism and racism, in her church and society. The first stage was her girlhood on the haciendas of Nepantla and Panoayán. The second stage was her life as a young adult in the vice regal court in New Spain as a lady-in-waiting. The third stage was her life as an adult nun living in the convent of Santa Paula.

The second section analyzes two primary texts written by Sor Juana in the first person—as noted, an unusual approach for this particular nun. They are *El Sueño* (*The Dream*) and *La Respuesta* (*The Answer*). Unlike Paz, who argues that Sor Juana's dream was written in 1685, I believe that it was written in 1688 or 1689 in response to two tragic moments in her life. The first was the death

---

1. Arenal and Powell, *Answer*, 16.

of her mother, Doña Isabel Ramírez de Santillana in 1688. The latter was the departure of her dear companion and patroness the *vireina* (vice queen), María Luisa, Marquise of Mancera, that same year. I analyze this poem in three sections. I hypothesize that this Baroque *silva* of nine hundred and seventy five lines, when viewed from a gender-specific lens, documents Sor Juana's her-story and experiences of inequality in all three stages of her life. Unlike *El Sueño*, where Sor Juana's cosmos is harmonious, reflecting God's reign in her social location, *La Respuesta* is a response to a living nightmare she endured at the hands of a misogynistic, patriarchal Jesuit cleric. Seen together the two texts juxtapose the dream of a more just world for disenfranchised persons in her region that included women and non-Spaniards.

Like Sor Juana, Latina feminists in the twenty-first century continue to endure the effects of patriarchy that shape systems of knowledge and social structures, secular and religious. In *El Sueño*, Sor Juana experiences noise as an evil that inhibits her from breathing fully. It denies her *libertad* (freedom) and her full humanity as a child of God. The question that follows for Latina scholars throughout the Americas today is both philosophical and anthropological. Its origins date to the colonial enterprise in Spanish America. The question revolves around what it means to be human. This is a central concern for Latina theologians in the U.S. and geopolitical South. In Sor Juana's colonial world it was the Spaniards who behaved in an inhumane and barbaric manner to the native population, the Nahua Mexica people. Their cultural legacy was the death of a civilization. In our own times the legacy of the conquest continues to be the focal point for U.S. Latina theologians' inquiries into our relationship with God, neighbor and non-human nature. In contrast to Spanish systems of knowledge U.S. Latina theologians' perspectives on God and the divine emphasize life. In the words of Sor Juana and subsequent U.S. Latina theologians, the greatest *fineza* (gift) of Christ was that He continues to walk with His people daily in *la cotidiano* (everyday life). Theirs is a renewed anthropology that is neither patriarchal nor androcentric, but embraces the diversity of all peoples and the cosmos, in contrast to the historical narrative of superiority that the Spaniards recounted upon their arrival into the Americas.

In 1974, Sor Juana was declared the first feminist of all the Americas. Today, in a similar vein, I claim that Sor Juana was not only an early feminist but an ecofeminist as well. In her 17th New Spain world, Sor Juana Inés de la Cruz's heightened sensitivity to injustice in her region was not limited to the issues of race, sex, and class but included as well a personal critique of Spaniards and non-Spaniards relationship to the land.

Acknowledgements

LIKE SOR JUANA INÉS de Cruz, I reflect the many individuals and relationships that have influenced me and made me the person I am today. Just as Sor Juana who identified herself as the daughter of Santa Paula, I too see myself as the daughter of Jeanne Marie Yugar, Mary Louise Ponnet, Norma Jordan, Lucy Saliba, Elizabeth Castro, Yvonne Mullaly, and Mary Boles. Similar to Sor Juana, in all three stages of my life, I have had a "vast throng" of women who supported me as a young girl, into my early adult years, and now. Sor Juana's *El Sueño* (*The Dream*) and *La Respuesta* (*The Answer*) reveal the powerful legacy of women in her life. In Sor Juana's *El Sueño*, the Great Goddess is prominent. She is Mother Earth. Her energy and life force ensure balance between human and non-human nature in the region. In my life the following women have served this important role: Rosemary Radford Ruether, Elisabeth Schüssler Fiorenza, Margaret R. Miles, Karen Jo Torjesen, Zayn Kassam, María Pilar Aquino, Sylvia Marcos, Sr. Gloria Marie Jones, O.P., Margaret Guider, O.S.F., Mary Hunt, Ivone Gebara, Riffat Hassan, Sandy Baldonado, Olivia Doko, Kathleen Mirante, and all the members of my Women Church Claremont group. In *La Respuesta*, Sor Juana creates a litany of women—Christian, pagan, and mythical—who were "good practitioners of know-ledge."[1] In my life these individuals are Rebecca Moore, Margaret Studier, Linda Vogel, Anne Eggebroten, Victoria Rue, Margaret Linnehan, Karen Kidd, Vivian Engel, Stephanie Glatt, and friends in the Immaculate Heart Community. At this point in my life I feel

1. Ibid.

Acknowledgements

connected to the final protagonist in Sor Juana's *El Sueño*, Atalanta. She is the woman warrior. She is independent and free. Her capabilities are equal to that of men. She symbolizes to me the individuals who remained steadfast with me along this journey. They are my *atrevidas hermanas*, "Daring Sisters," Jeanne Marie Yugar and Pamela Lynn Wasserman, who have not only been a constant source of strength to me but also are role models for me of strong and independent women who walk in the ways of wisdom, empowering individuals, male and female, along the way. They also are a community of scholars and activists who are also my friends. They have truly been my sisters in this process of giving birth to this manuscript. They are Diane Ward, Katherine Veach, Chase Knowles, Cynthia Bond, Matilde Moros, Ann Hidalgo, Kay Akers, Kathie Arscott, Jung Ja (Joy) Yu, Janice Poss, and Sarah Robinson. I am an echo of all of these women. In my life there have also been many men who supported my dream of achieving this goal. Among them are James, Frank and Chris Ponnet, Virgilio Elizondo, Luis Pedraja, Herman Ruether, Ramon Luzarraga, Gilberto Ruiz, Jorge Aquino, Paul Rodríguez, Juan Tavarez, Scott Wasserman, Rennie Truitt, Juan Castro Sr., Frank Castro, and José Quispe Castro. In a special way this *sueño* (dream) would not have come to fruition if it were not for the steadfast support of the following women in all of its stages. They are Rosemary Radford Ruether, Zayn Kassam and April Mayes, along with the Hispanic Theological Initiative, Joanne Rodríguez, Director, Angela Schoepf, kindred spirit, Ulrike Guthrie, editor, and Wipf and Stock, for their patience with me through this whole process. To all of these individuals, and others unnamed, I express my deepest gratitude.

SECTION I

Feminist Historical Reconstruction

CHAPTER 1

Introduction

GUSTAVO GUTIÉRREZ, FOREMOST LIBERATION theologian in Latin America, argues that the arrival of European conquerors in sixteenth-century pre-Hispanic America turned the "world inside out."[1] It was a "violent clash of thinking [between] Europeans [and] the spiritual world of the ancient Mexicans."[2] Prior to the encounter between the peoples of Spain and New Spain—now modern-day Mexico—the ancestors of the Nahua Aztec people lived in harmony with the land and its multiple ecosystems, and with their gods, goddesses and the cosmos. This *vieja civilización* (ancient civilization) spoke Nahuatl.[3] Its worldview was planetary and cosmocentric, which is to say it revolved around the earth, sky, clouds, rain, seeds and plants.[4] It was characterized by equilibrium, duality, complementarity, and balance.[5] The people of this ancient civilization respected the interrelatedness of all life forms, including animals, humans, and deities, male and female. The universe was not fixed or static but constantly changing.[6] For the Nahua people the earth was a celestial body.

1. Gutiérrez, *We Drink From Our Own Wells*, 11.

2. León-Portilla, *Aztec Thought and Culture*, 69.

3. Bernal, *Tenochtitlan*, 7.

4. Marcos, "Women's Religious Space in Mexico," 256.

5. Marcos, "Embodied Religious Thought: Gender Categories in Mesoamerica," 96–98.

6. Ibid.

In a three-year period, from 1519 to 1521, *conquistadors* (conquerors) from the Iberian Peninsula, more specifically Spain, changed all that.[7] Their presence on the continent disrupted the equilibrium and harmony that had existed in the region between the sexes, the land, the cosmos, the gods and goddesses, and human and nonhuman nature. Spaniards themselves testified that upon their arrival that this newly found territory was *un paradiso* (a paradise) or, *sueño* (dream).[8] Spanish rule turned this paradise into "a living hell for the natives."[9] The years that followed were a living nightmare. The colonial enterprise in New Spain was a watershed moment because it was the nadir of the subjugation of women and the indigenous population by outside forces.[10]

In Quechua, the indigenous language of the Incas in Peru, the word *pachacuti* literally means a "cosmic cataclysm."[11] Today it indicates hope for the restoration of the balance that was disrupted upon the arrival of Spaniards and others to Spanish America. *Pachacuti* points to the beneficial transformation of oppressive ideologies, social systems and structures that have historically denied the native population on the Latin American continent their full humanity as agents in their own right. In Spanish it is a *sueño*. In Nahuatl, the language of the Mesoamerican people, it is *temictli*. The dream, *sueño*, or *temictli*, embraces all of the inhabitants of the region, whether from in or outside of Spanish America's borders. Harmony on the continent can only occur if the two civilizations, Spaniard and the non-Spaniard, can recognize the beauty and ancient wisdom in each of their cultures.

Sor (Sr.) Juana Inés de la Cruz (1648/51–1695),[12] the seventeenth-century Latina philosopher and theologian, exemplifies one approach to this "cosmic cataclysm." In her time, as for the indigenous population, Sor Juana engaged in the work of trans-

7. Schwartz, *Victors and Vanquished*, 246.

8. Burkholder and Johnson, *Colonial Latin America*, 56.

9. Ibid., 44.

10. Ibid., 43.

11. Gutiérrez, *We Drink From Our Own Wells*, 11.

12. Paz, *Sor Juana*, 65.

4

formative change. Her life and writings critiqued patriarchal ideologies and social structures that denied the full self-actualization of the people in her social location, Spaniard, non-Spaniard, man or woman. For Sor Juana to achieve this *sueño*, she considered the epistemological question of what it meant to be human from both an anthropological and theological perspective. The realization of the dream demanded that the narrative and the oral traditions of her ancestors, the Mesoamerican Nahua people, be heard and affirmed by all people in her post-conquest world. Their cosmic worldview and belief systems needed to be reclaimed in their own right. In Sor Juana's her-story, the ancient wisdom of the Nahua people held the answer to harmony in her region and the epistemological question of what it meant to be human after the conquest.

In *El Sueño* (*The Dream*), Sor Juana refers to the conquest as *sacrílego rüido* (sacrilegious noise).[13] She does not identify the origins of the conflict but we can discern nuances in her dream as she ponders the two competing forces. From her personal experiences of sexism and racism, Sor Juana critiques patriarchal oppressive social systems, structures, and ideologies, but then widens the conversation to a larger consideration of this issue in the Church and her seventeenth-century society. Thus, Sor Juana's life and texts appear very feminist in that they move from the personal to the political. Central to her analyses is the exposure of the complicity of the Roman Catholic Church in the oppression and degradation of the indigenous population in Latin America.

In *La Respuesta* (*The Answer*), Sor Juana identifies women in the Christian tradition and the Church who used their education in the service of the Church. She mentions, a Gertrude, a Teresa, and a Brigid,[14] who through their studies served the Church in positive ways.[15] Sor Juana also notes, two native Mexican nuns,

---

13. Sayers Peden, *Sor Juana Inés de la Cruz*, 82.

14. I suspect Sor Juana's Gertrude and Brigid were saints, similar to Teresa, in the Christian tradition. If so, dates of birth and death for St. Gertrude are (ca. 1256–1302) and for St. Brigid (ca. 451–525). Mausolff, *Saint Companions*, 322, 9.

15. Arenal and Powell, *Answer*, 91.

one from the Convent of Regina and the other from the Convent of the Conception, who were respected by the Mexican theologian and Holy Scripture scholar, Dr. Juan Díaz de Arce (1594–1653).[16] The first for her mastery of the Divine Office and the other for her adept reading of the Vulgate Epistles which she eventually translated from Latin into Spanish.[17] In *La Respuesta*, Sor Juana asserts that Dr. Arce grieved the loss of the latter nun's life recognizing, "that such talents should . . . have been set to higher studies, guided by principles of science."[18]

Sor Juana includes a number of mystics in a catalog of noteworthy women as well. Although she does not name the Spanish woman, "the nun of Ágreda,"[19] Jean Franco, in her book *Plotting Women*, identifies this nun as María de Ágreda (1602–1665).[20] According to Franco, a Bishop José Ximénez Samaniego (1621–1692) validated De Ágreda's visions of the Virgin [Mary] as authentic and then had them published in a text entitled *Apología* (*The Apology*).[21] Another significant woman in Mexican religious history is Santa Teresa de Avila (St. Teresa of Avila, 1515–1582), a mystic, Church reformer, and important literary figure.[22] In *La Respuesta*, it is evident that Sor Juana had a deep respect for Santa Teresa, where she refers to her both in the singular and plural as "my own mother" and "Our Holy Mother."[23] I suspect that Sor Juana deeply admired Santa Teresa for two reasons. First, they shared a common heritage as Spaniards. Second, I think Teresa was a role model for Sor Juana as a literary figure and church reformer.

In contrast, Sor Juana did not include Santa Rosa de Lima (St. Rose of Lima, 1586–1617) in her litany of women.[24] Surely she

16. Ibid., 130.
17. Ibid., 93.
18. Ibid.
19. Ibid., 91.
20. Franco, *Plotting Women*, 28.
21. Ibid.
22. Arenal and Schlau, *Untold Sisters*, 1.
23. Arenal and Powell, *Answer*, 65.
24. Mausolff, *Saint Companions*, 244.

was familiar with this *mestiza* (racially mixed) woman's legacy in Peru, who in Sor Juana's lifetime was beatified and canonized a saint, by Pope Clement X on April 12, 1671.[25] In all of Spanish America Santa Rosa is recorded as the "most beloved of all Spanish American saints," and the only "American-born Roman Catholic to be declared a saint."[26] In Sor Juana's day, Santa Rosa de Lima was the model nun living a life of holiness, prayer, and penance. Was Sor Juana ambivalent about Santa Rosa, knowing that the canonization of this *mestiza* as a saint on their continent served the Church's patriarchal political agenda for women to be pure, modest, silent, and virtuous,[27] thus subservient to the Church and the Spanish Inquisition? My guess is that this was one reason for the timely manner in which her canonization process occurred.

I hasten to add that, unlike Santa Rosa de Lima who conformed to Counter Reformation standards for women, particularly nuns, the Church deemed mystics in New Spain especially suspect for their presumed affiliation with a group called the *alumbrados* (enlightened ones).[28] After the Council of Trent, 1545–1563, clerical leaders did not approve of this movement, neither in Spain nor in New Spain, because the female adherents of this group claimed their right to have a personal relationship with God outside of the confines of a patriarchal Church.[29] In Sor Juana's New Spain world, their refusal of the Church's teaching that it was the sole, "intermediary between mankind and God," was heresy, and grounds for punishment.[30]

Sor Juana, like the ancestors of the Nahua indigenous population in Mexican history, engaged in the "radical work," of turning the world right side up.[31] Her legacy rests in her reliance upon the anthropological wisdom of the Nahua Mesoamerican population

25. St. Augustine's Abbess, *Book of Saints*, 488.

26. Morgan, *Spanish American Saints and the Rhetoric of Identity*, 67.

27. Vives, *Education of a Christian Woman*, 132–136.

28. Lavrin, "Unlike Sor Juana?," 63.

29. Ibid., 64.

30. Ibid., 63.

31. Gutiérrez, *We Drink From Our Own Wells*, 11.

of her seventeenth-century region. The overriding question that guided this alternative epistemology and anthropology was how humans relate to neighbor, the cosmos and God. Unlike her male peers, Sor Juana experienced sexism and racism throughout her life. Her critiques emerged, therefore, in direct response to the inequalities and the devastation of ecosystems as she experienced it on the continent. Her legacy of resistance has been appropriated by Latina feminists today.

I desire to reclaim the dream of Sor Juana, for a more just and egalitarian world. I think it is possible because the ancient wisdom of her forebears, both women and men, modeled a worldview and life-giving ethic. In seventeenth-century New Spain, the Spanish Iberian worldview was the antithesis of a pre-Columbian worldview. In this book, I lift up Sor Juana Inés de la Cruz's *sueño* and legacy of resistance for a new generation to appreciate her quest for harmony for all peoples and civilizations under one g/God.

Methodology

This book constructs a holistic historical account of Sor Juana Inés de la Cruz's life and texts that engages all three stages of her life: her girlhood on the haciendas of Nepantla and Panoayán; her life as a young adult in the viceregal court in New Spain's capital, Mexico City, as a lady-in-waiting; and her life as an adult nun living in the convent of Santa Paula. It reconstructs Sor Juana's evolving awareness of inequalities in her region not only between men and women but also between Spaniards and non-Spaniards from a feminist perspective.

The challenge for all Sorjuanista scholars is that there are so many gaps in Sor Juana's personal narrative.[32] For biographical information, Sorjuanista literature relies heavily on the primary text, *La Respuesta*, dated March 1, 1691.[33] The reason for the reliance upon this particular text is not because of the wealth of informa-

---

32. Schons, "Obscure Points in the Life of Sor Juana Inés de la Cruz," 38.

33. Paz, *Sor Juana*, 414.

tion it holds about Sor Juana, but rather that it is one of the few sources of information about her interior life.[34] The task is all the more challenging for Sorjuanista scholars because the majority of Sor Juana's documents were written in the third person, making it difficult for scholars to discern Sor Juana's *propia* (own) voice in her texts.[35] In the words of Franco, the "I" in her texts is difficult to find.[36] Thus, the same basic details about Sor Juana's life are repeated over and over again. Truly trustworthy biographical information of Sor Juana is rare. Though *La Respuesta* is limited because it was written as a public defense against accusations made against her by a powerful church leader—and not specifically as autobiography, nevertheless, it remains an essential document because in Sor Juana's vast oeuvre of writings it provides glimpses into the challenges she endured in a largely patriarchal society in *sus propia palabras* (her own words). Sor Juana's *La Respuesta* is the starting point for this analysis, which is distinctive in its attempt to reconstruct a more complete account of Sor Juana's life-long sensitivity to the social inequalities in her world.

In this book, I examine Sor Juana's life through a feminist lens. I am interested in how patriarchal ideologies and institutions informed her critiques of the Church and societal norms prescribed for women of Spanish descent in the world of New Spain. I am also interested in the ways that social mores for women of Spanish descent in Spain and in New Spain shifted. Accordingly, I analyze primary and secondary documents, in Spanish and English, in an attempt to reconstruct a fuller biographical account of Sor Juana's life and the significance of communities of women that surrounded her in this process.

I analyze Sor Juana Inés de la Cruz's life and writings from a gender perspective employing two feminist methodological approaches. The first is Elisabeth Schüssler Fiorenza's feminist historical reconstruction methodology. The second is Rosemary Radford Ruether's feminist liberationist methodological approach

34. Salazar Mallen, *Una Biografía de Sor Juana Inés de la Cruz*, 9.
35. Franco, *Plotting Women*, 25.
36. Ibid.

with a shared sensitivity to ecofeminist concerns. Both Schüssler Fiorenza and Radford Ruether's methodologies deconstruct androcentric and patriarchal ideologies found in Scriptures, Christian history, and traditions. Schüssler Fiorenza's methodology is helpful in reclaiming and reconstructing Sor Juana's life and texts that have historically been discounted by patriarchal biases in the Roman Catholic Church in her seventeenth century world. Radford Ruether's methodological approach is useful in mining Sor Juana's life and texts for liberatory elements that can be used in creating a twenty-first century Latina feminist ecclesiology that can serve as the basis for an egalitarian Roman Catholic church and world.

For this study I define feminism and ecofeminism as follows. Feminism critiques patriarchal assumptions that women are inferior to men by virtue of their sex, while at the same time, advocates for the full humanity of women and men. Ecofeminism is a critique of patriarchal ideologies and assumptions that have resulted in the violation and domination of women and the earth. In this book, both terms are important as I argue that Sor Juana Inés de la Cruz, along with being the first feminist of all the Americas, is a prototypical ecofeminist as well.

In *Bread Not Stone: The Challenge of Feminist Biblical Interpretation* Schüssler Fiorenza argues that for centuries in the Christian tradition women have been silenced, leaving them without a written history or past.[37] In this way, data regarding women's role and significance in historic Christianity has been deeply skewed. She argues that, contrary to the "seeming evidence" that suggests that women were "insignificant," women were indeed significant, but overlooked as a result of a tilted patriarchal vision of authors in the past.[38] Schüssler Fiorenza asserts that in Christianity forces such as patriarchy, androcentricism and kyriarchy have marginalized not

37. Schüssler Fiorenza, *Bread Not Stone*, 102.

38. Schüssler Fiorenza's pioneering book, *In Memory of Her: A Feminist Theological Reconstruction of Christian Origins* states, "All historiography is a selective view of the past." She continues that all, "historical interpretation is defined by contemporary (and past, *my insert*) political interests and structures of domination." Schüssler Fiorenza, *In Memory of Her*, xvii.

only women but also all non-privileged White males.[39] Her interest is not only the liberation of women from "patriarchal religion and theology" but also all individuals who lack privilege and power and are consequently excluded by the winners of society from histories, stories, persons, and events.[40] Hers is a feminist critical hermeneutics of suspicion that examines Christian Scriptures, traditions, and texts from a liberative point of departure, not only for women, but also for all people who are oppressed by patriarchal power, ideologies and institutions.

Schüssler Fiorenza's scholarship is crucial for this study because it provides the medium for seeing Sor Juana Inés de la Cruz's life and texts, "in a different light and with different glasses,"[41] enabling the reconstruction of a more holistic account of Sor Juana's history and contribution in the Christian tradition. Utilizing a hermeneutics of suspicion, that begins with the presupposition that biblical texts and interpretations have historically been biased, androcentric and patriarchal, I will examine Sor Juana's life and texts in light of the culture she lived in, the system that maintained power in the hands of men, and perspectives that emphasized male superiority over females.

This book also relies upon Radford Ruether's feminist liberationist and ecological methodology to examine the intersection of patriarchy and sexism, and the violation of women and the earth in Sor Juana's social location, life and texts. Her methodology aids me in examining interlocking patriarchal systems of domination that oppressed Sor Juana, women, the Nahua population and the earth in seventeenth-century colonial New Spain. In this regard, Radford Ruether's assessment of patriarchy in the Roman Catholic

39. Schüssler Fiorenza defines kyriarchy as the "rule of the master or lord." She believes the word patriarchy, i.e., the rule of men, to be limited. She maintains historically not all men had power, but rather only "elite propertied men," through their roles as masters' to their wives and slaves. In her book, *But She Said: Feminist Practices of Biblical Interpretation,* she provides a visual paradigm which documents this seemingly democratic society rooted in a master/servant paradigm. Schüssler Fiorenza, *But She Said,* 117.

40. Schüssler Fiorenza, *Bread Not Stone,* 102.

41. Schüssler Fiorenza, *In Memory of Her,* xxiv.

Church is extremely relevant because the core of my analysis of gender discrimination in Sor Juana's life and texts has its origins in the Church as a colonial empire.[42] Similarly her critiques of Western colonialism, the origin of empires that began with the sixteenth-century colonial enterprise are just as important because both forms of patriarchy were interlocutors in Sor Juana's New Spain world.[43]

In a special way, Radford Ruether's methodology also affords me the opportunity to examine Sor Juana's unique contribution to the disciplines of feminism and ecofeminism. Sor Juana, like Radford Ruether, insists on the interdependence and interrelatedness of all life forms.[44] In Sor Juana words, she states that the "intricate structures of this world," human and nonhuman, "compose one single species."[45] Likewise, both critique patriarchy in its many manifestations. For Radford Ruether, it is dualisms between men and women, mind and matter, soul and body, that are the root cause of the domination of both women and the destruction of nature.[46]

Like Radford Ruether, Sor Juana mines Christian and non-Christian history, Scriptures and texts, myths, metaphors and narratives, for their liberative possibilities for humans but also all living bodies as well. Like Radford Ruether, Sor Juana rejects the ruling Iberian epistemology highlighting the liberative aspects of a Mesoamerican worldview as a model of "a more authentic ethic for ecological living" in her region.[47] In *La Respuesta* and *El Sueño* we see various ecofeminist themes. In *La Respuesta*, Sor Juana states that, "For although I did not study in books, I studied all the things that God created, taking them for my letters, and for my book all

42. Radford Ruether, *Christianity and Social Systems*, 11–24.

43. Radford Ruether, *Integrating Ecofeminism, Globalization, and World Religions*, 1–2.

44. Radford Ruether, *Gaia & God*, 48.

45. Arenal and Powell, *Answer*, 73.

46. Radford Ruether, *Sexism and God-Talk*, 78–79.

47. Radford Ruether, *Gaia & God*, 139.

the intricate structures of this world."[48] She continues "there is no creature, however lowly, in which one cannot recognize the great God who made me."[49] In *El Sueño*, Sor Juana's ecofeminist tendencies imbue all-aspects of her dream. In it, she creates a geocentric cultural universe rooted in a Mesoamerican cosmology that revolves around *La Naturaleza* (Nature), *la tierra* (the land), *la luna* (the moon), *el sol* (sun), *las estrellas* (stars), and *el cielo* (sky).[50]

Together, Schüssler Fiorenza and Radford Ruether's feminist methodologies lay the foundation for posing a number of fresh questions regarding Sor Juana Inés de la Cruz's life and texts. For example, many male theologians argue that theological interpretations are value-neutral, but along with Schüssler Fiorenza, I dispute this assumption.[51] Thus, it is necessary to view Sor Juana's life and texts from a gender-specific lens in order to create a more complete account of her life. The work of these two contemporary scholars provides the paradigm for investigating patriarchy in Sor Juana's time period, while at the same time offering the means for identifying liberatory aspects of her theological perspectives that can lay the foundation for a Latina egalitarian ecclesiology in the twenty-first century.

Historical Context

In the twentieth and twenty-first centuries, scholars representing diverse academic disciplines have been fascinated by the extensive body of work composed by Sor Juana Inés de la Cruz, which includes poems, plays, satires, carols, and theological treatises.[52] For more than three centuries after her death, the church to which she was devoted to suppressed her writings in an effort to erase her legacy from Spanish and Mexican history. In her own era, Sor

---

48. Arenal and Powell, *Answer*, 73.
49. Ibid.
50. Sayers Peden, *Sor Juana Inés de la Cruz*, 78, 86, 94.
51. Schüssler Fiorenza, *Bread Not Stone*, 98.
52. Arenal and Powell, *Answer*, 14.

Juana was a threat to the Church. She questioned clerical abuse of knowledge.[53] She challenged the premise that clerics were equal in status to God.[54] She disputed the theological assumption that women were incapable of engaging in intellectual discourses.[55]

By 1691, Sor Juana had upset the Church so much that the bishop of Puebla, Manuel Fernández de Santa Cruz (1637–1699), pressured her to sell her most prized possessions—one thousand to four thousand books, along with her scientific and musical instruments—and donate the proceeds to charity.[56] At the time, Sor Juana's library was the largest known in all of Spanish America.[57] It must have been a dim time for her.

Ten years earlier, in 1681, Sor Juana had challenged and dismissed Antonio Núñez de Miranda (1618–1695), inquisitor for the Church, as her confessor.[58] In 1693, it must have been extremely difficult for her to return to her previous confessor, who had declared her a "public scandal" in the region.[59]

Now, Sor Juana was alone and was forced to comply with prescribed norms for women of Spanish descent in a Counter Reformation world. At the time, she had no legal recourse or patron in the viceregal court or the Church to protect her from the torture presses of the Spanish Inquisition. I suspect tired and broken, Sor Juana bowed down to the Church in 1693, which maintained that it had the power to control her salvation.[60]

The Church that Sor Juana had served her entire life had turned on her. Suddenly, male prelates and priests made her feel like she was the cause of multiple natural catastrophes that were

53. Ibid., 81, 101.

54. Ibid., 41.

55. Ibid., 85.

56. Paz, *Sor Juana*, 398, 468.

57. Ibid.

58. The full title of Sor Juana's letter dismissing her confessor Núñez de Miranda is entitled, *Autodefensa espiritual, Sor Juana* (*Spiritual Defense, Sor Juana*). The full text is in Nina M. Scott's book *Madres del Verbo*, 71–82.

59. Arenal and Powell, *Answer*, 5.

60. Paz, *Sor Juana*, 459.

simultaneously occurring throughout the region (1691–1693).[61] Subsequently, on February 8, 1694, Sor Juana, "using blood from her veins as ink,"[62] signed a declaration of faith repenting of the alleged sins that supposedly had resulted in chaos in the region, by giving up her secular studies. Her signature was "I, Sister Juana Inés de la Cruz, the worst in the world."[63] The Church may not have tortured Sor Juana physically, but it did mentally and spiritually. It sold her lifeline, her books and scientific instruments.

In Sor Juana's world, the Church was patriarchal. It abused its power as clerics to force her to give up her life's work that was writing. It condemned her very nature. Upon her death, the Church burned Sor Juana's *papellitos* (writings), in this way suppressing her legacy in Mexico's history materially and metaphorically. If it were not for Alfonso Méndez Plancarte, who in 1952 retrieved and compiled Spanish translations of her works in *Obras Completas de Sor Juana Inés de la Cruz* (*The Complete Works of Sister Juana Inés de la Cruz*), and more recently, Octavio Paz's *Sor Juana, or The Traps of Faith*, published in 1988, the life and works of Sor Juana would continue to be unknown to the Spanish and English-speaking world.

Literature Review

In unraveling the gaps and multiple mysteries of Sor Juana's life an interdisciplinary approach is necessary to contextualize the scanty information we have about her life and social location. In the past twenty years various studies have provided new insights into the complexity of Sor Juana's genius, life, and texts in both Christian and Western history. These includes studies on the sixteenth-century Spanish Iberian colonial enterprise, the Counter Reformation, Medieval Christianity and mysticism, Spanish and Baroque Literature, and Mesoamerican spiritualities.

61. Schons, "Obscure Points in the Life of Sor Juana Inés de la Cruz," 54–55.

62. Leonard, *Baroque Times in Old Mexico*, 191.

63. Ibid.

Many Sorjuanista scholars, like myself, are drawn to Sor Juana's life and writings. These include: Electa Arenal, Alicia Gaspar de Alba, Luis Harss, Stephanie Merrim, Octavio Paz, Margaret Sayers Peden, Amanda Powell, Pamela Kirk Rappaport, George Tavard, and Alan Trueblood. These scholars, representing diverse disciplines, have illuminated the full implications of patriarchy and clericalism in Sor Juana's life and in the lives of Roman Catholic women more broadly. In Christian history, Sor Juana is one of many Latina women who have been denied their rightful place. In her times she was a prophet, a woman before her time, who like all prophets was met with resistance.

Two Sorjuanista scholars who have utilized their distinct research specialties to the study Sor Juana's life and writings stand out. The first is Reverend George Tavard's *Juana Inés de la Cruz and the Theology of Beauty: The First Mexican Theology.*[64] The second is Alicia Gaspar de Alba's *Sor Juana's Second Dream.*[65]

Tavard's book is particularly significant because he is the first scholar to reclaim Sor Juana as a theologian and analyze her writings from this perspective. While his treatise is a starting point, it is not an in-depth systematic analysis of the theological nuances in Sor Juana's work. To Tavard's credit, the publication of his book opened up a dialogue about Sor Juana's genius and her relationship to God and the Church that had been suppressed in Christian history. Moreover, his observation that the Roman Catholic Church and a U.S. English-speaking world have largely ignored Sor Juana's life and writings immediately gets to the heart of the matter.[66]

Tavard's work is also important because of his situation within the Roman Catholic Church as a cleric and theologian. Unlike women in the Church, Tavard's gender and status gave him the authority to advocate for Sor Juana to be recognized in Christian history as a female theologian of Spanish descent. In this way, the Assumptionist father reclaimed Sor Juana's contribution

---

64. Tavard, *Juana Inés de la Cruz and a Theology of Beauty*, 2.

65. Gaspar de Alba, *Sor Juana's Second Dream*, 1999.

66. Tavard, *Juana Inés de la Cruz and a Theology of Beauty*, 2.

in Christian, Spanish, and Western history as a woman theologian in her own right. Also distinctive to Tavard's perspective is his alignment with Sor Juana and her theological emphasis on the value and beauty of all creation, citing, for example, her words in *La Respuesta* that there is nothing in God's creation unworthy of being studied.[67]

Tavard's book opened up a space in theological discourse for a reflection on the significance of "A Theology of Beauty" in Spanish-speaking communities. Consequently, U.S. Latina/o theologians such as Alejandro García-Rivera, Roberto Goizueta, Michelle Gonzalez, and Cecilia González-Andrieu[68] are reclaiming a theology of beauty manifest in *la cotidiano* (everyday life) and the multiplicity of spiritualities of popular religiosities among varied Latina/o communities within the United States. Unlike Western conceptions of God that emphasize the omnipotence of God, U.S. Latina/o theologians reclaim a Christ-centered anthropology that embraces the beauty of God in all of creation. Like them, Sor Juana asserts the greatest demonstration of Christ's love is not that He "absented [H]imself from us," but rather that Christ is still "present in the transubstantiation of the Eucharist."[69] Tavard's work is considerable because it legitimates Latin American theological perspectives in the Church, many of which have been lost and are only recently re-emerging—including that of Sor Juana.

Unlike Tavard, who is a historical theologian, Alicia Gaspar de Alba is a feminist literary critic. Her novel, *Sor Juana's Second Dream*, is an important contribution to Sorjuanista studies. It provides a medium for non-academics to learn about Sor Juana. The title of Gaspar de Alba's novel is inventive, drawing upon the title of Sor Juana's *El Sueño*, published in Spain in 1692.[70] The full title was, *Primero sueño, que así intituló y compuso la madre Juana,*

67. Ibid.

68. García-Rivera, *Community of the Beautiful*, 1999. Goizueta, *Christ Our Companion*. Gonzalez, *Sor Juana*, 2007. González-Andrieu, *Bridge to Wonder*, 2012.

69. Paz, *Sor Juana*, 392.

70. Ibid., 357.

imitando a Góngora (First Dream, for Thus It Was Entitled and Composed by Mother Sister Juana, in Imitation of Góngora).[71] The title is significant because it hints at a comparison between Sor Juana's poem with the writings of the esteemed Baroque Spanish male poet of her times, Luis de Góngora y Argote (1561–1627).[72] Both Sor Juana and Góngora wrote a *silva*—a Baroque literary poem, with nine hundred and seventy-five verses.[73] Unlike Góngora, who wrote a second part to his poem entitled *Soledades* (*Solitary places*), it is a mystery as to whether Sor Juana wrote or would have written a second poem to complement her first poem, *El Sueño.*[74] Gaspar de Alba's novel is creative in that it builds on a historical precedent that remains a mystery to Sorjuanista scholars today. It also reinvents and reclaims Sor Juana's her-story at all three stages of her life. Her book is a good starting point for individuals who are new to Sorjuanista studies.

Gaspar de Alba's novel is particularly important to research into gender and sexuality in Colonial Latin American history. Her work provides the opportunity to analyze the multiple layers of sexual and social mores for individuals of Spanish descent in seventeenth-century New Spain. Gaspar de Alba's questions regarding Sor Juana's relationships to the *virreinas* (vice queens) in her life are quite valid. In the court, Sor Juana was surrounded by medieval conceptions of chivalry that included romanticized love between ladies-in-waiting and knights who playfully engaged in varied relationships, sexual and non-sexual. Sor Juana's poetry reinvents courtly literature to frame women in a positive light, elevating their beauty to that of the divine. This included elevating the *virreinas* on earth to Mary, the *virreina*, "Queen of Heaven."[75]

71. Ibid.

72. Ibid.

73. Ibid.

74. Ibid., 356.

75. Kirk Rappaport, *Sor Juana Inés de la Cruz*, 173, 47. For Sor Juana, Mary is "Sovereign Queen of Heaven," the "Princess Immaculate," and "Supreme Empress of the Angels." She is also *Tota Pulchra*, translated in Nahuatl as, "most beautiful." Mary, like her people, is also "Black." Sor Juana confirms this referencing the Song of Songs, Chapter 1:5–6. In a similar fashion, Leonor

Gaspar de Alba's feminist perspective on Sor Juana's writings are a medium to raise questions about women and sexuality in both historical contexts. It has opened up space for a dialogue on sexuality in her era and ours. Asunción Lavrin's book entitled *Sexuality & Marriage in Colonial Latin America* on women and sexuality during this time period is a wonderful supplement to Gaspar de Alba's novel. In it, Lavrin describes the range of sexual practices that were normative in Sor Juana's time. They included premarital sexual relations, homosexuality, polygamy, bigamy, and out-of-wedlock births,[76] between religious and laypersons.[77] Lavrin further observes that sexuality and marriage need to be understood within the context of prescribed sexual norms for individuals in the Church and the reality of popular practices of the people at the time.[78] Paz would concur with Lavrin, as he avers that, "we must modify our ideas about seventeenth-century morality . . . [where] [s]exual orthodoxy was much less rigorous than religious orthodoxy."[79]

I agree with Tavard that there needs to be room in Sor Juana's poetry to recognize the empathy she had for all women in her lifetime.[80] Further, I agree with Paz who asserts that Sor Juana's appreciation of women and subsequent "defense of women cease[d] to be opinion," but rather was "a moral, even visceral reaction to lived

---

Carreto (1664), María Luisa, Countess of Paredes (1680), and the Countess of Galve (1688) are the *virreinas* (vice queens) on earth. To describe them, Sor Juana uses secular sources, primarily Greek and Roman mythic figures. They are "Venus," "the brightest of all the planets," and "natural objects in the night sky." In Sor Juana's world these women are, "Harmony," "Proportion," and "Beauty."

76. The distinction between religious and laypersons is that the former is ordained in the Church while the latter is not. In the Roman Catholic Church though nuns take similar vows to male priests including poverty, chastity and obedience, men are exclusively ordained.

77. Lavrin, "Sexuality in Colonial Mexico," 48.

78. Ibid.

79. Paz, *Sor Juana*, 68.

80. Tavard, *Juana Inés de la Cruz and a Theology of Beauty*, 13.

experiences."[81] Thus, Gaspar de Alba's novel, *Sor Juana's Second Dream*, is important because it provides a constructive medium through which to interpret Sor Juana's interior life, while at the same time it invites other scholars and non-scholars to learn more about Sor Juana's texts and life.

Structure

The first is a Feminist Historical Reconstruction of Sor Juana Inés de la Cruz's life and texts. The second section is a Feminist Textual Analysis of two documents Sor Juana uniquely wrote in the first person. The first is *La Respuesta*, simply translated as *The Answer* and *El Sueño*, translated as *The Dream*. My intention is two-fold: first, to mine Sor Juana's writings for critiques of established norms for women in the Roman Catholic Church and her seventeenth-century New Spain society at each stage of her life; and second, to unearth elements of liberatory feminist and ecofeminist principles that will lay the foundation for a Latina Liberative Ecclesiological paradigm in the twenty-first century.

To achieve this end I will integrate the methodological underpinnings of Elisabeth Schüssler Fiorenza and Rosemary Radford Ruether. These include the following:

1. The intersection of her social location and her criticism of inequalities in her seventeenth-century New Spain world;

2. Secular and religious texts that informed prescribed social norms for men and women in her times; and

3. Elements of her works that could potentially be used as a liberatory paradigm for a renewed church and world in Latin America today.

In Chapter 2, I provide an overview of three historical moments that are relevant to the intersection of Sor Juana's life, writings, and the gender discrimination that she experienced at each

81. Paz, *Sor Juana*, 68.

stage. It is not meant to provide an in-depth historical analysis of these select moments. Rather, utilizing a gender-specific lens it allows for a fuller understanding of sexism as Sor Juana experienced it in her lifetime. The first significant social indicator is the sixteenth-century encounter between Spain and New Spain, or modern-day Mexico. The second is the importance of the Reformation and Counter Reformation Movement in Spain and, subsequently, Mexico. The third location is shifting norms for women of Spanish descent in Spain and Mexico after the Counter Reformation Movement, particularly as they relate to the Spanish Inquisition and women's deviance from orthodox behaviors stipulated for women in Spanish America.

In Chapter 3, four sections follow that comprise a feminist historical reconstruction and analysis of Sor Juana's family of birth, life as a young girl, a young adult, and as a mature adult. In each section I explore Sorjuanista literature, in English and in Spanish, for allusions to significant women in her life, along with gender-related issues that informed Sor Juana's attitudes regarding distinctions between the sexes.

In Sorjuanista studies the intersection of the historical context with events in Sor Juana's life have not been researched extensively. I can understand why it is difficult for Sorjuanista scholars to re-create or re-construct the lives of women in Spanish America. For the most part patriarchal readings have denied women's agency and contributions within Christian history. Paz's minimal assertion that Sor Juana grew up surrounded by spirited and enterprising women is one example of that.[82] It fails to bring these various women to life. Though his book on Sor Juana is commendable for bringing her life and texts across the border into a North American context it is still a reductionist statement about the significance of women in Sor Juana's life.

My role as a feminist historian is to reconstruct and reclaim not only Sor Juana's her-story but also that of the women around her whose her-stories have also been overshadowed by patriarchal biases. These women include Sor Juana's mother, her maternal

82. Ibid.

grandmother, her full and stepsisters, the *virreinas* and the community of sisters she lived with for twenty-five plus years.

The second section of this book—Chapters 4, 5, and 6—is a feminist analysis and close reading of two of Sor Juana's above-mentioned primary texts. I intentionally chose these documents for the task of illuminating Sor Juana's life because they were written in the first person and thus reflect her *propia* voice. The documents complement each other in several key ways. The first is a theological treatise. The latter is a poem. They complement each other in that both are personal testimonies of Sor Juana's experiences of sexism in her world. The first is personal while the latter is political. Both testify to the vulnerability of women who chose to resist orthodox patriarchal standards prescribed for them in secular and religious spheres.

In the concluding chapter, I analyze recurring themes in Sor Juana's life and texts as they relate to her understanding of patriarchy. I consider them as resources for the creation of a twenty-first century Latina Ecclesiology of Liberation. In *La Respuesta*, Sor Juana re-interprets classical Church dogma and doctrine so that the authentic origins of the Scriptures and Christian tradition and history are liberative for all people and the earth too. In *El Sueño*, Sor Juana draws on Mesoamerican thought along with Roman and Greek classical mythic figures to symbolically discuss her own struggles to overcome patriarchy and inequalities in her seventeenth-century world, in all three stages.

I hypothesize that Sor Juana is not only a precursor feminist but also an ecofeminist philosopher and theologian. Though chastised by clerics and the Church in her time, Sor Juana continued to work for a "cosmic cataclysm," the transformation of patriarchal structures, in both the Church and Spanish Inquisition.

Final Reflection

In the twenty-first century, no Sorjuanista scholar can claim their commentaries on Sor Juana's life and works are definitive or value-neutral.[83] Much of Sorjuanista scholarship reflects the personal biases and projections of individuals who have used her and her writings to support their arguments. For example, Gaspar de Alba argues that Sor Juana was a lesbian. Paz assumes that Sor Juana was psychologically impaired due to the absence of a father figure in her life. Ludwig Pfandl suggests that Sor Juana's life and texts mirror Sigmund Freud's psychoanalytical theory of the Oedipal complex.[84] And, like many other Sorjuanistas that include Electa Arenal, Stephanie Merrim, Margaret Sayers Peden, Amanda Powell and Pamela Kirk Rappaport, I believe Sor Juana's life and texts echo principles of a feminist agenda applicable to contemporary times.

Sor Juana Inés de la Cruz challenged the Church to be more authentic to Jesus' mission of inclusivity of all people, Christian, non-Christian, pagan, non-pagan, indigenous, *mestizo* and black. For her, each had a place in Christian salvation history. In her lifetime, she bridged different cultures and worldviews. She did so by tapping into the wisdom of her foremothers and forefathers, the Nahua Mesoamerican people, whose worldview affirmed life, earth and the cosmos in its totality. Unlike Church orthodoxy that placed high value on an omnipotent God, Sor Juana attested that God is ever-present in *la cotidiano* of God's people. In her lifetime, Sor Juana bridged a Spanish and Mesoamerican worldview. Her legacy is that she united a global Church and world through an ecofeminist perspective safeguarding life for all peoples and for Earth, Herself. Her life and thought contribute to the formation of a liberative Latina ecclesiological paradigm based on a holistic understanding of a God who is not only all-knowing but who also accompanies God's people daily, *diriamente*.

83. Schüssler Fiorenza, *Bread Not Stone*, 98.

84. Paz, *Sor Juana*, 67.

CHAPTER 2

The Historical Context for Understanding Sor Juana's Her-Story

Introduction

TO BEGIN SOR JUANA Inés de la Cruz's her-story, I will provide an overview of three historical moments that are relevant to the intersection of her life, writings, and the gender discrimination that she experienced at each stage. They are the sixteenth-century colonial enterprise in Spain and New Spain, the Protestant and Counter Reformation movements in Spain and New Spain, and the prescription of gender roles for women in the Iberian Peninsula and their transmission into Spanish America. This historical review will aid us in identifying recurring themes Sor Juana addresses in her writings, paying particular attention to positive influence of the indigenous wisdom of the Nahua Mesoamerican people. Octavio Paz's insight on Sor Juana Inés de la Cruz's significance in Mexico's history is telling. He asserts:

> Both life and work unfold within a given society and thus are intelligible only within a given society; at the same time, its history would not be what it is without the life and works of Sor Juana. It is not enough to say that Sor Juana's work is a product of history; we must add that history is also a product of her work.[1]

1. Paz, *Sor Juana*, 4.

The Sixteenth-Century Colonial Enterprise in Spain and New Spain: 1500–1650

To cross the threshold into Sor Juana's seventeenth-century historical moment, one must situate the relationship between Spain and the inhabitants of New Spain prior to the arrival of Spanish Europeans in 1519. Davíd Carrasco, Miguel León-Portilla, and Octavio Paz concur that this cultural encounter between two civilizations was a brutal clash of two cosmovisions.[2] In a three-year period, 1519–1521, Spanish *conquistadors* destroyed the landscape of the Aztec or Mexica Empire and the capital, Tenochtitlan.[3] Depending on who is narrating the story of the encounter, it could be framed as a positive or negative event. Contrary to the reports of the historical narrative written by the victors in history, the Mesoamerican society into which Sor Juana was born was a highly sophisticated and developed civilization with its own military, governmental, and religious systems. Distinctive from Spain, which desired homogeneity and *limpieza de sangre* (purity of blood),[4] New Spain was ethnically, racially, culturally, and linguistically diverse. Prior to the arrival of European Spaniards in Spanish America an estimated eighty million individuals inhabited the region; by 1500, that number was reduced to an estimated twenty-five million native persons; and in 1550, the number had decreased to ten million.[5] Most of the native peoples were of Aztec ancestry and spoke Nahuatl. By the seventeenth century, what had once been a densely populated territory of native individuals had decreased to an estimated one million.[6]

2. Carrasco, *Religions in Mesoamerica*, 129. León-Portilla, *Aztec Thought and Culture*, 69. Paz, *Sor Juana*, 14. See Schwartz, *Victors and Vanquished*, for primary documents of the encounter between Spain and modern-day Mexico from a Spanish and a Mesoamerican indigenous perspective.

3. Schwartz, *Victors and Vanquished*, 127.

4. Twinam, "Honor, Sexuality, and Illegitimacy in Colonial Spanish America," 123.

5. Carrasco, *Religions of Mesoamerica*, 129.

6. Ibid.

In Sor Juana's era, the African presence in the colonized territory was dominant over the indigenous population.[7] Spaniards could no longer exploit natives as servants or slaves, due to the papal bull *Sublimis Deus* (*The Sublime God*) outlawing Indian enslavement promulgated by Pope Paul III in 1537.[8] *Sublimis Deus* "proclaimed the human status of Indians and their right to freedom and ownership, while reproving the violence committed against them."[9] Slavery, harsh treatment, disease, and malnutrition, had resulted in widespread death. In response, Spaniards sought other resources to further their colonial agenda of Spain to establish settlements and develop natural resources in the region. The result was a new wave of trading that brought in Africans as slave laborers. Individuals of African descent represented fully fifty percent of the population in New Spain by the seventeenth century.[10] Sor Juana thus grew up acutely aware of the distinctions between the Indigenous, Spanish, and African cultures and ideologies.

In New Spain, imperialism left a legacy of cultural, religious, and ideological repression in an encounter between two dominant cultures and two very distinct ways of knowing. The first was a Mesoamerican worldview while the latter was Spanish. A major distinction between these two epistemologies is that one is cosmocentric and the other is human-centric. In Mesoamerican religious thought the world revolves around the cosmos: the sun, moon, and stars, plants, animals, humans, space, and time.[11] Life is understood along a continuum.[12] Binary oppositions are nonexistent.[13] Parity between gods and goddesses, the sexes, and human and nonhuman nature is understood as part of a divinely

---

7. Bennett, *Africans in Colonial Mexico*, 7.

8. Gutiérrez, *Las Casas in Search of the Poor*, 302–308.

9. Ibid., 175.

10. Bennett, *Africans in Colonial Mexico*, 9.

11. Marcos, "Mesoamerican Religions," 654–655.

12. Marcos, *Taken from the Lips*, 21.

13. Ibid., 22.

ordained cosmos that is regenerative and sustained by human's relationships to the gods.[14]

In contrast, a Spanish Iberian epistemology reflects an ethos of European philosophical traditions such as Platonism and Aristotelianism. These traditions understand the world in dualistic terms, such as male and female, mind and body, and human and nonhuman nature.[15] In Spanish America dualisms informed the status of Spanish and non-Spanish individuals, nuanced by variables such as race, sex, and class, but also ethnically stratified hierarchical distinctions between them.[16] Unlike the Mesoamerican cosmovision, the Spanish Iberian epistemology centers on the human person, a singular male God, and the written word.

In Sor Juana's Mexican world, as is the case in many colonial settings, the Spanish epistemology was considered more civilized than the indigenous wisdoms of ancestral peoples.[17] Nevertheless, Sor Juana valued the multiple ways of knowing that she was exposed to which were reflected in the *mestizaje* and the blending of the Nahua and Spanish culture/civilizations after the conquest. Indeed, she was an example of this blending. She was creole (a Spaniard born in the New World) but also culturally *mestiza* (an individual of biracial, Spanish and indigenous, descent).[18] In one poem, it is quite evident that Sor Juana identified as Mexican, which included both her Spanish and Mesoamerican heritage. She asked, "*¿Que mágicas infusiones de los indios herbolariosde mi Patria, entre mis letras el hechizo derramaron?*"[19] In English, "What magic infusions of the Indian herbalists of my country spread the magic spell over my literary works?"[20]

During Sor Juana's lifetime, the landscape of a once sustainable pre-Hispanic region radically changed from an ecologically

14. Marcos, "Mesoamerican Religions," 654–655.

15. Radford Ruether, *Sexism and God-Talk*, 78–79.

16. Socolow, *Women of Colonial Latin America*, 60.

17. Burkholder and Johnson, *Colonial Latin America*, 53, 133.

18. Ibid., 413.

19. Williams and Rodriguez, *Sor Juana Inés de la Cruz: The Tenth Muse*, 2.

20. Ibid.

communal-centered ethic to one that was individual-centered, to the detriment of the environment.[21] Native-born Spaniards not only exploited the land and native population, but also the varied ecosystems that sustained *la cotidiano* in Sor Juana's world. In her writings, exploitation of women and the land are recurring themes. In *El Divino Narciso* (*The Divine Narcissus*), for example, she transforms Ovid's famous *Metamorphoses* into a love story between God and humanity.[22] In Ovid's text, the character Narcissus is self-centered. By contrast, in Sor Juana's drama, Narcissus takes the form of Jesus who looks into a fountain and is awed by beauty in humanity and all of creation.[23] The content of this drama echoes an ecofeminist epistemology and anthropology that affirms that all creation is beautiful, made in God's image and likeness. Her interpretation proposes an alternative Christian anthropology to that of Iberian Christians and Spaniards, one that reveres all living entities including human and nonhuman nature, and the cosmos.

Ten years into the colonial enterprise in New Spain sexual, physical, and verbal abuse characterized the Spanish conqueror's relationship to inhabitants there.[24] Nahua women suffered more than their male counterparts at the hands of Spaniards, who violated their bodies and thereby disrupted the cultural universe of Mesoamerican people.[25] In Nahua culture, the phrase used to describe this sacrilegious behavior is the de-flowering of their women.[26] The reality was that at the time, *Peninsulares* (Spaniards born in the Iberia) had left their wives behind in Spain, and engaged in immoral behavior in New Spain.[27] In response, the Church and Spanish Crown decided to establish settlements in Sor Juana's region, in the hope that an influx of women of Spanish descent would minimize sexually immoral behavior by male Spaniards in

21. Sanders and Price, *Mesoamerica*, 69–73.

22. Gonzalez, *Sor Juana*, 75.

23. Ibid.

24. Socolow, *Women of Colonial Latin America*, 53–54.

25. Burkholder and Johnson, *Colonial Latin America*, 196.

26. Poma de Ayala, *First New Chronicle*, 123.

27. Socolow, *The Women of Colonial Latin America*, 53.

New Spain. They also hoped that the migration of Spanish women from the Iberian Peninsula would facilitate the process of populating New Spain with European Christian offspring, introducing Iberian cultural values into newly conquered territories.[28] As a result, the arrival of Spanish women reached a high point of thirty to forty percent of all immigrants by the end of sixteenth century.[29] This number is striking given that in the early 1500s only about one thousand European women of Iberian Spanish descent had immigrated to Spanish America.[30] In Sor Juana's world, however, the presence of Iberian Spaniards was at its highest, an estimated twenty-eight to forty percent of all residents of New Spain at the time were from Spain.[31]

Unlike the early years of the conquest that were characterized by widespread violence and bloodshed, the society in which Sor Juana grew up saw the Nahua population oppressed in new ways. In their attempt to maintain loyalty to the Spanish Crown and the Church, Spaniards imposed regulations on non-Spaniards in the region. In both Spain and New Spain the Spanish Inquisition played a significant role in controlling conquered peoples, creating bureaucratic systems, regulating behaviors, determining racial hierarchies, and exploiting territories, peoples, and natural resources. This market-economy justified Spanish superiority over other peoples and cultures.

In Sor Juana's lifetime, inquisitors were ever-present in social and religious institutions. The viceregal court and the Church were highly structured to maintain Spanish rule in New Spain.[32] In New Spain, these institutions monitored fidelity to the Spanish Crown and those powerful Catholic monarchs in Europe who were connected to Spain and the Catholic Church. Together, these institutions sought to monopolize territories and evangelize

---

28. Ibid., 54.
29. Ibid.
30. Ibid.
31. Ibid.
32. Schwartz, *Victors and Vanquished*, 127.

conquered persons to convert to Christianity, the dominant religion in Europe.

In 1521, Spanish rule forcibly imposed its political and religious agendas on the predominantly Nahuatl speaking population of the region.[33] Not only did Spaniards colonize the land of Sor Juana's New Spain, they also colonized the minds and belief systems of native persons, thereby denying their humanity and voice in the public sphere. Spaniards were the privileged minority who were granted authority by the Spanish Crown and Church to enforce a rigid, racially segregated, hierarchically stratified society based on color, ancestry, gender, and class.[34] This social hierarchy allowed the Spanish Crown and the Church to maintain a tight hold on their privileges and powers through directly and indirectly ranking a person's ancestral heritage.

Spaniards established a colonial economy based on castes.[35] In Sor Juana's lifetime, Indians, Africans, American-born descendants and racial mixtures were hierarchically stratified as inferior to Spaniards from Spain.[36] Gender and racial markers informed a person's status as well, often privileging the Spanish elite aristocracy at the expense of the Nahua indigenous majority. European Spaniards from the Iberian Peninsula were deemed the superior race.[37] Spaniards born in the Americas were creoles, second in this caste system. Individuals of a mixed race followed and included people of Spanish, Indian, and African descent. They were *mestizos, mulattos,* and *zambos.*[38] In New Spain, native individuals, slaves, wage laborers, maids, artisans, and merchants were ranked lowest in this color-based stratified society, and were referred to as *castas.* In Sor Juana's world, they were the most vulnerable to exploitation and discrimination through political and religious regulatory laws established by Spaniards born in the Americas.

33. Burkholder and Johnson, *Colonial Latin America,* 133.

34. Schwartz, *Victors and Vanquished,* 1.

35. Burkholder and Johnson, *Colonial Latin America,* 196.

36. Ibid.

37. Ibid.

38. Ibid.

Sor Juana enjoyed the privileges of being a daughter and grand-daughter of Spaniards in Mexico and Spain. Her status as creole afforded her privileges denied to non-Spaniards.

In Sor Juana's day, Mexico City was the center of public life. It was structured to maintain Spanish rule and power in the region. Spanish architecture reflected Iberian social attitudes of superiority in both rural and urban settings.[39] It was rectangular in design and mirrored the Spanish architecture in Madrid.[40] In the name of the Spanish Crown, governmental institutions, the viceregal court and the Church were situated in the center of the *traza* (plaza).[41] The minority elite class lived near it in the center of the capital city while the majority of the population lived outside of Mexico City in rural regions. The hierarchy established by the Spanish Crown fueled animosity between individuals native to the region and the invading Spaniards. Their cultural universe, belief systems, and sacred objects were both defiled and under scrutiny by the Spanish Crown.

Sor Juana was exposed to these conflicts and contrasts: first in the rural setting on the haciendas of her birth and youth and later in the urban setting of Mexico City as a member of an elite aristocratic caste. In colonial Mexico the hacienda of Sor Juana's birth and youth was a microcosm of a macro colonial society that reflected a multiplicity of hierarchies. Unique to Sor Juana's her-story is that she lived in both settings. Thus, she experienced the sharp disparities between these two worldviews. The caste systems, ideologies, and institutions that privileged some at the expense of others heightened her consciousness of the hierarchies that shaped and informed her world. It seems likely that Sor Juana would have been acutely aware that the hacienda her mother managed would not have functioned if it were not based on a hierarchical system that included slaves: black, white, and *mestizos*. These experiences were formative in the development of Sor Juana's assessment of the widespread inequalities in seventeenth-century New Spain, as can be seen in her writings.

39. Ibid., 252.
40. Ibid.
41. Ibid.

The Protestant and Counter Reformation
Movements in Spain and New Spain

The Protestant and Counter Reformation movements in Spain and New Spain significantly influenced the lives of women of Spanish descent in Sor Juana's lifetime. In the Church's attempt to regain its power it emphasized, "the retention of Catholic dogma,"[42] emphasizing utopian values based on "traditional doctrine[s]."[43] Christian spiritual practices were regularized, stressing prayer and the spiritual exercises, the cult of the Virgin Mary and saints, and the role of the Church as intermediary between humanity and God.[44] Nuns were required to have a male confessor.[45] In the process, the Church adopted strict regulations concerning sexuality, marriage, and prescribed social norms for women of Spanish descent.[46] Thus these movements are significant in Sor Juana's her-story because they coincide and shape key moments in her life, origins, and familial situation in New Spain.

The upheavals generated by the Reformation fueled intense efforts to create a perfect vision of a pure Church. Deviance of any kind from traditional, orthodox Church ideals was deemed suspect. The re-publication of Heinrich Kramer and James Sprenger's, *Malleus Maleficarum*, in English, *The Hammer of [Female] Witches*, first published in 1486, set the stage for the Spanish Inquisition in Spain and New Spain. This manual—designed to identify witches through torture and ordeal—became the justification for persecuting individuals, primarily women, who did not subscribe to orthodox church teachings and values. Women healers, possibly *curanderas* in Sor Juana's world, were particular targets of the Inquisition.[47] In Spanish America, it is documented that women

---

42. Kidd, *Counter-Reformation*, 55.

43. Burkholder and Johnson, *Colonial Latin America*, 64.

44. Lavrin, "Unlike Sor Juana?," 64.

45. Ibid.

46. Socolow, *Women of Colonial Latin America*, 13–15.

47. Sánchez Ortega, "Woman as Source of 'Evil' in Counter Reformation Spain," 198.

were accused, investigated and killed for heresy seventy-five percent more often than men.[48] Everyone, especially those connected with the Church, were well aware of the consequences of not conforming to prescribed social codes for women in the Church and the colonial world. Christian believers would have heard stories and seen women burned at the stake under the charge of witchcraft, when their real crime was simply deviating from prescribed norms. To be brought before the Spanish Inquisition evoked images of torture, death, purgatory, and hell, for the Christian, and we find that torture and persecution are recurring themes in Sor Juana's writings.

Prescription of Gender Roles for Women in the Iberian Peninsula and their Transmission into Spanish America

During the sixteenth and seventeenth centuries prescribed patriarchal gender roles for creole women in New Spain collided with matriarchal influences within the Mesoamerican tradition that believed in equality of both sexes. Gender roles for women of Spanish descent were influenced by a multiplicity of ideologies, secular and religious, many of which restricted women's agency to the private sphere. In Europe, Platonic and Aristotelian thought began to dominate Spanish culture. As a result, Greek philosophies and church doctrines overlapped and created a cultural universe for women characterized by dualisms and hierarchies. Religious constructs elevated men to the transcendent higher-level rational mind, while women were relegated to a lower status, associated with body, matter, and nature.[49] For the Church this meant that maidens and decent ladies lived under the custody of a male figure whether it was a husband, father or brother.[50] In Spain and New Spain a woman's honor now depended on her subservient status to a male figure. The only socially acceptable choices available

---

48. Ibid.
49. Radford Ruether, *Sexism and God-Talk*, 93–94.
50. Socolow, *Women in Colonial Latin America*, 11–12.

for women in this new environment were either to marry or to enter the convent. Being single was not an acceptable choice for a woman of Spanish descent.

This marked a clear change in attitudes about sex and sexuality as a result of the Reformation. Though society was gendered in Spain, prior to the Counter Reformation, sex in and of itself was not demonized. After the Counter Reformation, however, sex was sinful outside of marital contracts.[51] In this process virginity became connected with a woman's honor. While it is important to highlight that in every society social mores for individuals are not clear-cut, nonetheless a distinction must be made between the idealized behavior for men and women in contrast to the lived realities of the people.

During Sor Juana's lifetime the new gendered norms for women in New Spain were difficult to preserve, particularly with regards to a woman maintaining a virginal state.[52] The colonial enterprise, from the beginning, brought with it an outlook of conquest, not only of land, but of women as well. Because there was no accountability for the men not to violate women in Spanish America, it became a common practice, and this practice continued in Sor Juana's lifetime. In Spanish America, in the name of the Spanish Crown, Spanish men felt entitled to conquer the indigenous population, their land, and women that inhabited the land. Indigenous persons were considered dispensable. They endured harsh working conditions, enslavement, and abuse by Spanish conquerors.[53] Spaniards considered themselves to be the superior race in contrast to the indigenous peoples they conquered, and so women were particularly vulnerable to Spaniards' violation of their bodies.[54]

This violation is reflected in Sor Juana's famous poem, *Hombres Necios* (*Foolish Men*) and in *La Respuesta*, where she addresses the misogynistic attitudes towards women while at the same time

51. Ibid., 13.

52. Schons, "Obscure Points in the Life of Sor Juana," 43.

53. Burkholder and Johnson, *Colonial Latin America*, 43–44.

54. Ibid.

advocating that all women be educated. She asserts, "Oh, how many abuses could be avoided in this land if only the women were educated."[55] Sor Juana's underlying assessment of gender relations is that even within the confines of women being educated they were also vulnerable to abuse by men. In this, she may well have been influenced by her mother, Doña Isabel Ramírez, who chose to remain a *soltera* (single woman) and not marry Sor Juana's biological father.

I suspect Sor Juana's maternal grandparents, Pedro Ramírez de Santillana and Beatriz Rendón, probably lived in Spain prior to the Counter Reformation. In the Ramírez de Santillana household, it seems likely that Doña Isabel's choice to be single and have children outside the confines of marriage had significant repercussions for her as a woman in New Spain. This violated the Counter Reformation ideal that women remain under the control of men, either as married women or as professed religious women.[56] Sor Juana's mother's choice to be *soltera* and not enter into a formal marital contract allowed her to retain full control over financial assets that would have been relinquished to her husband if she had married.[57]

Both Sor Juana and her mother Doña Isabel opted out of a life in which they were under the control of a man. They were both deviant and daring in their choice to remain single and not to marry. Sor Juana and her mother, as members of a semi-elite class, did have more options in making the choice to be single in contrast to women of lower classes and of non-Spanish descent. Nevertheless, their resistance to newly-imposed restrictions upon women are noteworthy.

55. Arenal and Powell, *Answer*, 91.

56. McHugh, O.P. and Callan, O.P., *Catechism of the Council of Trent*, 342–345.

57. Socolow, *Women of Colonial Latin America*, 12.

Conclusion

This chapter has laid the foundation for a feminist historical reconstruction of Sor Juana's life. The variables elaborated above were the sixteenth-century colonial enterprise in Spain and New Spain, the Reformation and Counter Reformation movements in Spain and New Spain, and the prescription of gender roles for women in the Iberian Peninsula and their transmission into New Spain. In the following chapters we will see that shifting attitudes with regards to women as a result of the encounter between these continents would shape prescribed gender roles for women of Spanish descent into which Sor Juana was born. In New Spain, the Church and the Spanish Crown played a key role in Sor Juana' critiques of prescribed social and sexual norms for women. The following chapters will continue this analysis in light of the variables defined above with the expectation that these historic moments might help me to reconstruct a fuller picture of the intersection of Sor Juana's life and writings and of her subsequent choice to be a single woman in her society as a professed religious.

Sor Juana Inés de la Cruz Family Tree

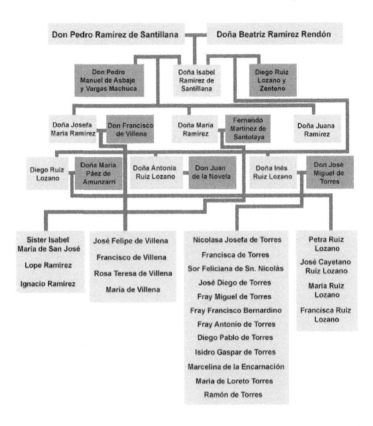

CHAPTER 3

A Feminist Historical Reconstruction of the Biography of Sor Juana Inés de la Cruz

Introduction

JUANA RAMÍREZ DE ASBAJE, most remembered by her professed name, Sor Juana Inés de la Cruz, was born in a colonized territory a little more than a hundred years after the initial encounter between Spain and Mesoamerica, in 1519. In her lifetime, she lived in three communities of women where she was exposed to varied inequalities between the sexes, Spaniards and non-Spaniards, and the indigenous peoples who, at the time, represented the majority. In Sor Juana's lifetime, New Spain was a stable global empire governed predominantly by Spaniards born in the Americas.[1] Sor Juana's family was of Spanish descent, and her mother and father, along with her siblings and half-siblings, were born in the Americas, and thus were creoles, *criollos*. In the caste system, created by Iberian Spaniards after the conquest, native-born Spaniards were the elite minority. Sor Juana's biological father and grandparents were members of this class. Her family members held respectable professions indicative of their caste: landowners, clerics, nuns, members of the military, administrators in Mexico City's prominent university, and civil servants for the Church and state.[2] They also enjoyed privileges denied to non-Spaniards that

1. Sabat-Rivers, "A Feminist Re-reading of Sor Juana's Dream," 142.
2. Paz, *Sor Juana*, 67–69.

included leasing property from the Church and holding positions of authority in secular and religious settings.[3]

At three stages in her life, Sor Juana was significantly influenced by participating in communities comprised of women. The first was as a young girl in a household of seven women that included two full and two step-sisters, along with her mother Doña Isabel Ramírez de Santillana and maternal grandmother Doña Beatriz Ramírez Rendón.[4] The second was as a young adult when Sor Juana lived in the viceregal court in New Spain's capital Mexico City as a lady-in-waiting for five years (1664–1669). In the court, Sor Juana's patronesses included three *virreinas* (vice queens) who paralleled the three stages of her life: Lenor Carreto, Marquise de Mancera (1664–1673); María Luisa Manrique de Lara y Gonzaga (1680–1686); and María Elvira de Toledo, Countess of Galve (1688–1696).[5] The third stage was as a mature adult and nun, when she lived in the convent of Santa Paula under the auspices of Sr. Andrea de la Encarnación, the *Priora*, or prioress of Sor Juana's convent.[6] In these varied communities, women informed Sor Juana's perspectives on inequalities between the sexes, Spaniards and non-Spaniards and individuals of varying ethnic backgrounds, social classes, and religious affiliations.

This feminist reconstruction of the life of Sor Juana Inés de la Cruz will take into consideration the intersection of these communities of women and the themes that emerge in all three stages of her life. I argue these communities of women helped to shape Sor Juana's evolving indictment of patriarchal norms, social structures, and ideologies for women in both the public and private spheres.

---

3. Burkholder and Johnson, *Colonial Latin America*, 252.

4. Paz, *Sor Juana*, 67–68.

5. Schons, "Obscure Points in the Life of Sor Juana Inés de la Cruz," 38.

6. Cervantes, *Testamento de Sor Juana*, 50–51.

Her Family of Birth

Sor Juana was the daughter of Doña Isabel Ramírez de Santillana (?–January, 3, 1688), and Don Pedro Manuel de Asbaje (fl. 16th cent.).[7] She grew up in a single-parent household, by choice or chance, one cannot know for sure. Little is known about Sor Juana's father. Georgina Sabat de Rivers verifies that he was a Spanish captain from the Basque region in Spain.[8] In Sor Juana's will of February 23, 1669, she does state that her biological father was *difunto* (deceased) and that she was the legitimate daughter (*hija legítima*) of Pedro de Asbaje and Isabel Ramírez.[9] Sor Juana continues, *Sea notorio a los que el presente* (It is well-known to everyone here) that this assertion is true.[10] It therefore appears that Sor Juana knew her paternal father and that he may have lived in the region. If he did, Sor Juana most likely resented him because he had denied her and her full sisters legitimacy by not recognizing them as his own. Their illegitimate status stained their virtue and honor in the eyes of the Church and her seventeenth century New Spain society.[11] Sor Juana communicates this sadness in a poem. In English the poem translates as follows: "Not to be born of an honorable father would be a blemish, I must own, if receiving my being from no other I had not known it was his alone. Far more generous was your mother when she arranged your ancestry, offering many a likely father among whom to choose your pedigree."[12] In Spanish, the poem reads as follows.

> *El no ser de Padre honrado,*
> *fuera defecto, a mi ver,*
> *si como recibí el ser*
> *de él, se lo hubiera yo dado*

7. Ramírez-España, *La Familia de Sor Juana Inés de la Cruz*, 57.

8. Sabat-Rivers, *Sor Juana Inés de la Cruz*, 10.

9. Cervantes, *Testamento de Sor Juana Inés de la Cruz*, 16.

10. Ibid.

11. Twinam, "Honor, Sexuality, and Illegitimacy in Colonial Spanish America," 123.

12. Paz, *Sor Juana*, 66.

Más piados fue tu Madre,
que hizo que a muchos sucedas:
para que, entre tantos, puedas
tomar el que más te cuadre.[13]

In Sor Juana's world, her illegitimate status was also mitigated by her mother's prominent leadership role in the community. In Spanish America, a person's illegitimate status could be formally re-evaluated based on other variables, including a person's positive participation in public life. To Sor Juana's advantage, her mother was a respected woman of Spanish creole descent, in both the public and private sphere. She was a hacienda owner, an enterprising profession for a woman in her century. She was also the head matriarch of the Ramírez de Santillana familial kinship. Though Sor Juana's mother could have gone through the available legal process to have her children deemed legitimate, she chose not too. Instead, in Doña Isabel's will of 1687, she identifies all of her children as illegitimate, without apology.

Growing up, Sor Juana had two full sisters, Josefa (fl. 16th cent.) and María (fl. 16th cent.), along with two stepsisters, Antonia (1658–?) and Inés (1659–?), and a stepbrother, Diego Lozano (1656–?). Sor Juana's only brother was from her mother's second partner, Diego Ruíz Lozano, a lance captain who was affiliated with the European Spanish military.

Sor Juana's date of birth is not known conclusively. Two archival documents, one secular and one religious, suggest Sor Juana was born in 1648 or 1651, respectively.[14] The first document was Doña Isabel Ramírez's will that dates to 1687.[15] The second document, from Fr. Diego Calleja (?–1725), Sor Juana's friend and biographer, claims that Sor Juana was born on November 12, 1651.[16] There are no other legal documents to confirm either date. Most Sorjuanista scholars agree that Sor Juana was born in 1648 because a parish registry of San Vicente, in the region of

13. Scott, *Madres del Verbo,* 88.

14. Paz, *Sor Juana,* 65.

15. Ibid.

16. Wissmer, *"El amigo español de Sor Juana,"* 377–388.

Chimalhuacán, reveals that a young girl named, "Inés," was baptized on December 2, 1648.[17] Sorjuanista scholars presume this young girl was Sor Juana Inés de la Cruz, although it might be the birth information of her step-sister Inés. The child's godparents were Doña Isabel Ramírez's sister and brother, Beatriz (fl. 16th cent.) and Miguel Ramírez (fl. 16th cent.).[18] These documents are important because in Sor Juana's era children born out of wedlock were often not recorded in the church's registry. Most likely, Sor Juana's status as *criolla* influenced the documentation of her birth. In a European Spanish framework that desired homogeneity among members of New Spain society, children deemed illegitimate, whether of Spanish or non-Spanish descent, were treated in different ways.

Little is known about Sor Juana's mother, Doña Isabel Ramírez or grandmother, Doña Beatriz Rendón. Paz's account of the women in Sor Juana's life is brief. He asserts that Sor Juana grew up in a household of strong, spirited, and enterprising women.[19] His comment does not do justice to the significance of these woman, not only in the Ramírez family, but in Sor Juana's wider community. Like many women in Christian history, the her-stories of Doña Isabel Ramírez and Doña Beatriz Rendón have been lost. In spite of these challenges, the following facts are known about Sor Juana's mother and her grandmother.

First, Doña Isabel Ramírez (?–1688) was the mother of six children, most notably identified with don Pedro de Asbaje, the father of her renowned daughter Sor Juana Inés de la Cruz. Second, Doña Isabel was the daughter of esteemed landowners, Don Pedro Ramírez de Santillana (?–1666) and Doña Beatriz Rendón (?–October, 1657), who in her lifetime leased two estates from the Church.[20] Third, Doña Isabel, upon the death of her father, Don Pedro Ramírez de Santillana, in 1665, assumed the position of

---

17. Paz, *Sor Juana*, 65.
18. Ibid.
19. Ibid.
20. Vallejo de Villa, "*Acerca de la loa*," 80–81; 118.

43

head administrator of the Ramírez de Santillana estates.[21] Lastly, though apparently illiterate, Doña Isabel was a resourceful, intelligent and enterprising woman.[22]

The following facts can be gleaned from Paz's biographical text with regards to Sor Juana's grandmother, Doña Beatriz Rendón. First, Doña Beatriz was born a Spaniard, but moved from Spain to New Spain sometime before the Counter Reformation movement in Europe.[23] Second, Doña Beatriz, like her husband Don Pedro Ramírez de Santillana, came from the region of Andalusia, Sanlúcar de Barrameda in Spain.[24] Third, Doña Beatriz and her husband were hacienda owners, leasing property from the Church in the Central Valley of Mexico, then New Spain.[25]

It is apparent that these maternal figures exercised significant influence over the children, stepchildren, and grandchildren in the Ramírez de Santillana kinship household. Sor Juana and her siblings grew up observing that women were just as intelligent and capable as men of taking on leadership roles in the public and private spheres. Their mother was a prime role model. Doña Isabel, not only provided for the well being of her children but also governed two estates leased to her family by the Church for more than thirty years.[26] It was a feat that earned her mother respect. The first estate was in Nepantla where Sor Juana was born. The second was in Panoayán, a *pueblo* (town) near Amecameca where Sor Juana grew up.[27] For five generations after the death of her grandfather, the women in the Ramírez de Santillana kinship network administered this land. By not marrying, Doña Isabel

21. Paz, *Sor Juana*, 65.
22. Ibid.
23. Ibid., 67.
24. Ibid.
25. Ibid., 65–68, 154.
26. Ibid., 67.
27. Ibid., 65.

kept the monetary value and assets of the land within the Ramírez de Santillana family.[28]

Upon Doña Isabel Ramírez's death, in 1688, she passed on the administrative responsibility of this land to her daughter Doña María Ramírez.[29] Sor Juana may have been asked by her mother to relieve her full sister, María, as administrator of these estates but she evidently declined. Unlike María, who had a household to manage, including three children and her husband, Sor Juana was single. More importantly, Sor Juana had the skills to manage the Ramírez de Santillana's haciendas successfully. Sor Juana's desire to study and pursue her education outweighed her interest in taking on the responsibility of her family's assets. Sor Juana's stepbrother, Diego Ruíz Lozano, evidently took over the lease, breaking the legacy of the Ramírez de Santillana administration of these estates.[30] Under his leadership the lease to this land was not renewed by the Castilian monarchy, an interesting gender twist in the patriarchal society of New Spain. Diego may not have been not successful in managing both estates because he lacked the skills to be a hacienda owner. He was trained by his father to be a military captain, not an administrator. Unlike Sor Juana and her two full sisters, Josefa and María, Diego did not witness their mother's leadership in this capacity. At the time of his birth, Sor Juana's mother was older and thus less likely to have passed on these skills to him.

Life as a Young Girl (1648–1661)

Sor Juana had limited access to books as a child. Thus, her curious nature, imagination, and experimentation were mediums to learn about the world around her. In her own words, Sor Juana states that the world was her textbook.[31] Sor Juana's philosophical inclinations began in the playground and kitchen. Each space pro-

---

28. Socolow, *Women of Colonial Latin America*, 10.
29. Paz, *Sor Juana*, 67–68.
30. Ibid.
31. Arenal and Powell, *Answer*, 75.

vided her a forum for social scientific inquiries and self-directed discovery. In the kitchen, Sor Juana hypothesized about the relationship between the egg and the yolk and how and why it separated when the eggshell cracked. Her inquiry led her to ascertain that an egg became solid when cooked in oil and butter and dissolved in sugar syrup.[32] On the playground, Sor Juana was fascinated by the "spherical form" and "momentum" of a top and how it responded to gravity.[33] This led her to order a child—probably a *mestiza* child, the daughter of the hired help—to bring her flour so that she could sift it onto the floor and observe whether the top's motion continued to make perfect circles or spiraled as it lost its momentum.

From an early age, Sor Juana was audacious and conniving. In *La Respuesta*, she asserts that she was nearly three years of age when she pleaded with her mother to enroll her in a school for young girls called *Amigas*.[34] Her mother's response was that she was too young. Still, Sor Juana testifies that she followed one of her older sisters, either Josefa or María, to the school. She told the teacher that her mother had given her permission to be there though this was not true. Sor Juana claims that the teacher, "to humor my whim . . . gave me lessons."[35] To the teacher's surprise Sor Juana learned how to read before her mother found out that she was attending the school.

Sor Juana heard there was a university in Mexico City where she could study the sciences.[36] She writes that she dressed up in men's clothing pleading with her mother to send her to the capital to live with some relatives so that she could enter and study at the University.[37] Although Doña Isabel refused, she did send her daughter to live with her maternal grandmother and grandfather on the family's second hacienda in Panoayán, in order to appease

32. Ibid.
33. Ibid.
34. Ibid, 49.
35. Ibid.
36. Ibid.
37. Ibid.

her precocious daughter's pleas. Her grandfather, Don Pedro Ramírez de Santillana,[38] had a personal library where he studied. Sor Juana reports that her mother was right to do this, because "she quenched [her] desire by reading a great variety of books that belong[ed] to [her] grandfather."[39]

The move turned out not to be an ideal one for Sor Juana. Life on her grandparents' hacienda was not conducive to learning. Her grandparents had eleven children and their families lived there as well.[40] Along with them, there were house slaves living in or around the home.[41] It was noisy, to say the least. There was a constant bustle of activity in the household. In this setting, Sor Juana created mischief for her grandparents. No doubt she was a precocious grandchild. This is most likely why in *La Respuesta*, Sor Juana testifies that, "neither punishments nor scoldings could prevent me [from studying]."[42]

By age six or seven, Sor Juana knew how to read, write, embroider and sew.[43] It was during this time too that she won a prize from the Church for a *villancico* (carol) she wrote in celebration of the Holy Eucharist.[44] The song Sor Juana wrote at such an early age probably appeared in the style of the *villancico* sung by the native persons in her region.[45] She must have heard the songs of the Nahua population as they remembered and celebrated historical moments, such as the conquest and the cyclical nature of the earth and their relationship to god. In contrast to the Nahua population, that celebrated the sun God, Huitzilopochtli, she celebrated Jesus, the Son of God.[46] Her genius was noted by authorities and she received a gift from the Church for this song. I believe that the Church did

38. Paz, *Sor Juana*, 67.

39. Arenal and Powell, *Answer*, 51.

40. Brandenburg, *Sor Juana Inés de la Cruz*, 83.

41. Ibid.

42. Arenal and Powell, *Answer*, 51.

43. Ibid., 59.

44. Merrim, *Feminist Perspectives on Sor Juana Inés de la Cruz*, 15.

45. Arenal and Powell, *Answer*, 149.

46. Nicholson, *Mexican and Central American Mythology*, 91.

not make the connection between Sor Juana's *villancico* and the Nahua population in her region from whom she had learned this style of poetry. Unlike the Church, Sor Juana was able to shift, mix, and blend the faith traditions of her region with ease.

As a young girl, Sor Juana probably was exposed to schools created specifically for indigenous children. In the Nahua culture, boys and girls were equally educated. In class, students learned the history of their people through the written word and song. For the Nahua people, it was extremely important for all of their children to know their history, oral traditions, songs and stories. These schools pre-dated the conquest. Ferdinand Anton states:

> One of the most important achievements [of the Mexica people] was the introduction of compulsory education. The date when this was done cannot be ascertained exactly; that it happened was a tremendous achievement for that time. In the Medieval Ages, when in Europe school education was a privilege of the upper classes; there was in the Aztec society not a single child, of whatever origin, who grew up without it. The state took care of the education of children. With immense solicitude it tried to further civilization, to uphold morals, and to train useful subjects.[47]

In her youth, Sor Juana may not have been able to fully articulate or analyze her experiences; nevertheless, I think they laid the foundation for her later writings and remonstrances against inequalities based on a person's race, sex, or social status. The presence of women and the Nahua population made more of an impression on her than the presence of men. Although the idea of patriarchy as oppressive to women did not exist in the seventeenth century, seen through a twenty-first-century lens, patriarchy permeated all aspects of Sor Juana's life and texts. In the next two stages of her life we will see that she uses her *pluma*, or pen, as a medium for civil resistance to normative standards for women in her society.

47. Anton, *Women in Pre-Columbian America*, 211.

Life as a Young Adult (1661–1669)

Sor Juana moved to Mexico City when she was thirteen. Perhaps bored because she had reached the end of educational opportunities in the nearby town, Sor Juana once again pleaded with her mother to move to Mexico City to live with her mother's full sister María de Mata (fl. 16th cent.).[48] This time, her mother agreed and Sor Juana moved to Mexico City. It is likely that she travelled there in a boat on one of the causeways, or canals, that were used by the indigenous people to sell their goods in the capital.[49]

The Ramírez de Santillana family belonged to a small elite class of individuals of Spanish descent in the region.[50] Like her mother, she was addressed with respect as Doña Juana Ramírez. There, she was under the protection of her mother's sister, Doña María Ramírez, who had married Don Juan de Mata, a wealthy aristocrat, who had close ties to the viceregal court.[51] In the Mata home, Sor Juana enjoyed a comfortable lifestyle surrounded by maids of different castes—indigenous, black and *mestizos*—as she studied in their private library. Living in this setting provided Sor Juana with numerous opportunities to socialize with members of this elite group, and eventually she would be invited to live within the viceregal court by the then viceroy and vice queen.

Sor Juana's two full sisters, Josefa and María, and stepsister, Inés Ruiz Lozano, also lived in Mexico City. Each of them had married Spaniards. Sor Juana, through her stepsister Inés and her husband José Miguel de Torres (fl. 16th. cent.), the then-secretary of the local university, was able to take independent lessons, in Latin, from a professor affiliated with that university.[52] In *La Respuesta*, Sor Juana comments that she mastered Latin in fewer than twenty lessons.[53] It may not have been Sor Juana's first exposure

---

48. Paz, *Sor Juana*, 51.
49. Gomez, *La Ruta de Sor Juana*, 8.
50. Paz, *Sor Juana*, 67.
51. Ibid.
52. Ibid.
53. Arenal and Powell, *Answer*, 51.

to this ancient language. In 1528, "only seven years after the fall of the Aztec capital," a Nahuatl document entitled, *Unos anales históricos de la nación Mexicana* (*Some historical annals of the Mexican nation*), was translated not only into Nahuatl but also into "the Latin alphabet."[54]

For the Nahua population of Sor Juana's region, the Conquest was a significant moment in their history and thus needed to be documented in written form.[55] Contrary to dominant narratives that the indigenous population in Spanish America relied solely upon oral tradition, this was not the case. In *Mexican and Central American Mythology*, Irene Nicholson argues that the written word was just as important to the Nahua people.[56] For Sor Juana's ancestors, both oral stories and texts were mediums to document philosophical and religious ideas that cherished "the unity of all knowledge."[57] Sor Juana's appreciation of the wisdom of all disciplines and cultures, particularly as it related to understanding more about God and the divine in her world, may have had its origins in a Nahua ethic of knowledge.

In 1663, at age sixteen, Sor Juana formally met the viceregal couple Don Antonio Sebastián de Toledo and his wife, the *virreina* Doña Leonor Carreto, Marquise de Mancera.[58] The couple was drawn to Sor Juana's personality and the versatility of her knowledge. That same year she moved into the viceregal court as a lady-in-waiting. Though formally under the patronage of the viceregal couple, in the court Sor Juana was Doña Leonor's protégée.[59] For two years, Sor Juana lived in this highly aristocratic environment where the privileged elite enjoyed life amidst the riches that their social class afforded them. In the court, the *virreina* nurtured her intellectual capacities as a young writer and scholar. There, Sor Juana's self-confidence grew as her public recognition and fame

54. León-Portilla, *Broken Spears*, 154–155.

55. Ibid.

56. Nicholson, *Mexican and Central American Mythology*, 10.

57. Ibid.

58. Paz, *Sor Juana*, 88

59. Franco, *Plotting Women*, 24.

spread throughout the region for her defense of women's right to be educated. I think that Sor Juana's disregard for men grew as well as she saw how they toyed with women's emotions in the royal court.

Sor Juana found her literary voice in the royal court. She artfully wrote poems and plays that celebrated women and critiqued established norms for men and women. It was during this time period that Sor Juana wrote her most provocative poem: *Hombres Necios.*[60] In it, she disputes the patriarchal assumption that women were irrational and argues instead that it was men who were both foolish and irrational.[61] She makes this daring declaration, "Thus I prove with all my forces the ways your arrogance does battle: for in your offers and your demands we have devil, flesh, and world: a man."[62] This poem undoubtedly became a topic of discussion in both religious and secular settings, especially among clerics such as her confessor Antonio Nuñez de Miranda who was "the guardian of doctrine" as "censor for the Holy Office."[63]

As a young woman, Sor Juana was a threat to Church orthodoxy, as can be surmised from later conflicts between her and the Church. Those in the Church could not rebuke her for her nonconformity to prescribed religious norms for women because the viceregal court was equal in power and authority to them. In the court, Sor Juana was free to study, think, and write on secular and religious themes. In her young adult years, she was not as fearful of challenging the ecclesial establishment. In the second and third stages of Sor Juana's life, however, her conflicts with the Church intensified. In her youth, Sor Juana had been the church's pride, recognized widely throughout the region for her gifts and talents. But during her adult life, Sor Juana's relationship to the Church became more complicated.

---

60. Arenal and Powell, *Answer*, 157, 159.

61. Ibid.

62. Ibid.

63. Paz, *Sor Juana*, 450.

Life as a Mature Adult (1669–1695)

In 1669, at age seventeen, Sor Juana, like other maidens of her era, needed to choose a socially acceptable profession for a woman of her status. She had two life options: to marry or enter the convent.[64] Both professions secured a woman's status, social respectability, economic security, and salvation. Unlike her mother and grandmother, who in a pre-Counter Reformation world had the option to be single, at Sor Juana's time that was not a respectable vocation for a young woman. To be a nun or married within one's caste was highly recommended, in both Spain and in Spanish America.[65] Both life choices reflected a post-Counter Reformation agenda for women to be placed under patriarchal control. Both these two life choices required a dowry, which Sor Juana did not have.[66]

Because a woman's virginity distinguished a woman's status and virtue, this explains why there were so many convents in New Spain. Paz estimates that there were more than twenty-five convents in Mexico City in Sor Juana's lifetime, each of which catered to a woman's rank and social status.[67] There was even a rebellion of women in the region who demanded that the local bishop invest money in creating more convents to safeguard women's virginity and honor.[68] Women of all ranks and castes needed to safeguard themselves against aggressive and belligerent men if they were to secure their salvation. The male element of the population was under no restraint (even the priesthood was no exception) and men roamed at will, preying upon women: Not only immorality, but depravity and beastiality reigned. Therefore, a woman's honor and virginity were important considerations when choosing a life profession. As a nun, a woman was respected as a bride of Christ.[69]

64. Lavrin, "Unlike Sor Juana?," 62.

65. Socolow, *Women of Colonial Latin America*, 59–61.

66. Paz, *Sor Juana*, 118.

67. Ibid., 117.

68. Schons, "Obscure Points in the Life of Sor Juana," 41–43.

69. Socolow, *Women of Colonial Latin America*, 90.

In contrast, in marriage a woman was destined to a life of servitude to her husband.[70]

Though Sor Juana was a member of a semi-elite class, Paz writes that her family was of moderate means.[71] This statement raises questions for me. It seems that Sor Juana did not have a financial safety net when she was discerning her future either to be a professed nun or to get married. Though the Ramírez de Santillana family was of some means, the land they leased from the Church did not necessarily make sufficient profits. Moreover, dowries for nuns were not cheap. To enter the novitiate as a nun in the seventeenth and eighteenth centuries, the convent expected dowries that were from "two thousand to four thousand pesos," depending on the social class of the convent.[72] To marry, dowries ranged from "one thousand to five thousand pesos."[73] If a woman entered the convent the dowry was expected immediately, "generally deposited in cash," while if a woman chose to marry the delivery of the dowry could be delayed by virtue of "a lien on a family's properties."[74] Sor Juana's financial situation would be a consideration for her in discerning her life profession.

In Sor Juana's discernment process she was resolute about two things regarding her life-long profession. First, marriage was not an option. Thus, Sor Juana, like her mother, chose a lifestyle in which she would not be under the direct control of a man. Second, Sor Juana, like other women of her times, was also deeply concerned about the salvation of her soul.[75] Unlike most Sorjuanista scholars, I want to emphasize the latter part of the following statement because other scholars overlook it. I think Sor Juana's salvation was of equal importance to her life choice as a single woman. She writes:

70. Ibid., 67.
71. Lavrin, "Unlike Sor Juana?," 62.
72. Ibid.
73. Ibid.
74. Lavrin, "Sexuality in Colonial Mexico: A Church Dilemma," 62.
75. Lavrin, "Unlike Sor Juana?," 62

> I took the veil because, although I knew I would find in
> religious life many things that would be quite opposed to
> my character (I speak of accessory rather than essential
> matters), it would, given my absolute unwillingness to
> enter into marriage, be the least unfitting and the most
> decent state I could choose, with the assurance I desired
> of my salvation.[76]

Encouraged by her confessor Antonio Núñez de Miranda, Sor Juana ultimately decided to be a nun. It is said that in Sor Juana the Church had won one of the most celebrated ladies in all Mexico. Sor Juana entered two different convents as a novice. The first was the convent of San Jose, which belonged to the Order of the Discalced Carmelites.[77] Then, and now, it is known as *Santa Teresa de Antigua* (Saint Terese the Old).[78] Sor Juana probably entered this convent for three reasons. First, unlike other convents, it did not require a novice to bring a dowry.[79] Second, she also had a special respect for Santa Teresa whom she mentions in *La Respuesta*, as, "Our Holy Mother" and "my own mother" too.[80] Third, like Santa Teresa, she was of Spanish descent and a reformer in the Church. In three months, however, Sor Juana left due to illness.[81] The ascetic life of the Carmelites proved too difficult for Sor Juana who had lived in privileged and pampered settings her whole life. From there, she went back to the viceregal court where she recovered during the course of a year.[82]

Sor Juana then entered the convent of San Jerónimo and Santa Paula where she would spend the rest of her life. If not for the sponsorship of Don Pedro Velázquez de la Cadeña, Sor Juana would not have been able to cover the expenses of entering this convent

76. Lavrin, "Sexuality in Colonial Mexico: A Church Dilemma," 51.

77. Ibid.

78. Ibid.

79. Lavrin, "Unlike Sor Juana?," 62.

80. Arenal and Powell, *Answer*, 65.

81. Ibid., 6.

82. Brandenberg, *Sor Juana Inés de la Cruz*, 96–97.

suitable to her caste.[83] It was compatible with Sor Juana. It was a convent for women of her social class, as *criolla*.[84] In this setting she could pursue her studies in a relaxed environment and not have to worry about her day-to-day needs such cooking, cleaning, and the maintenance of sleeping quarters. In her times, nuns had maids and slaves who catered to their everyday needs, depending on their social class.[85] Upon entering this convent, Doña Isabel, Sor Juana's mother, gave her a mulatto slave, who with Sor Juana enjoyed the benefits of a two-story cell, bathroom, kitchen, and a sitting room, along with sleeping quarters.[86] She lived with Sor Juana until she became pregnant and was then sold to her sister Josefa.[87]

Within the walls of the convent Sor Juana was highly regarded and appreciated. There she used skills she had learned from her mother in service of her convent. For a total of nine years, Sor Juana was re-elected twice as archivist and treasurer for the entire religious community.[88] In this capacity, she was on the congregational council with the head prioress, Sr. Andrea de la Encarnación.[89] Sor Juana, like her mother, was a businesswoman and entrepreneur. Sr. Andrea recognized this and thus chose her to oversee the convent's financial resources for two terms.[90] Her entrepreneurial skills were not limited to the convent but were also used in family-related situations.

Though isolated within its walls, Sor Juana was very much aware of what was going on outside. When her eldest full sister Josefa was abandoned by her husband, Sor Juana helped her to financially secure a hacienda in the Chalco region.[91] She also defended the legal rights of her niece, her older sister María's daugh-

83. Paz, *Sor Juana*, 118–119.
84. Ibid.
85. Ibid.
86. Ibid., 120.
87. Cervantes, *Testamento de Sor Juana*, 21.
88. Paz, *Sor Juana*, 121.
89. Cervantes, *Testamento de Sor Juana*, 21.
90. Paz, *Sor Juana*, 121.
91. Ibid., 68–69.

ter, Isabel María de San José (fl. 16ᵗʰ cent.), from her step-nephew
Francisco de Villena (fl. 16ᵗʰ cent.), step-son of Josefa, who wanted
to claim her niece's assets as his own.[92] In her final years Sor Juana
was concerned about the future and financial security of her protégée and abandoned niece, now Sister Isabel María de San José, and
did enormous amounts of paperwork on her behalf.[93]

Sor Juana's relationship with her confessor, Núñez de Miranda was stormy over the years. At first, they were collegial, even
though it was well known in the region that he was a misogynist.[94]
Then he became her opponent. In public he said she was a scandal
in the Church.[95] Despite her grief at his comment she was bold
and responded to his public condemnation of her. In 1681, at
thirty-three years of age, Sor Juana responded in a letter entitled,
Autodefensa espiritual: Sor Juana Inés de la Cruz (*Spiritual Defense:
Sister Juana Inés of the Cross*).[96] In it she asked why he hated her so
much, and suggested that if he could not say anything respectful
about her and her nature it would be best to relieve him of his du-
ties as her confessor, which she did.[97] This must have enraged him.
This anger toward her I suspect was also shared by the community
he belonged to, the Society of Jesus, the most powerful clerics in
New Spain at the time.

Eventually Sor Juana returned to her confessor Núñez de Miranda and lived a life of penance according the standards for nuns
after the Counter Reformation. Sor Juana had served the court and
convent for more than twenty years, writing poetry, sonnets, letters, *villancicos*, and plays for the two leading political powers of
her time: the vice-royal court and institutional Church. Among
the many documents she wrote at the request of these two institutions were: *Tres Sonetas sobre la Muerte de Laura, 1674* (*Three
Sonnets on the Death of Laura*); *Villancicos de San Pedro Nolasco,*

92. Ibid.
93. Cervantes, *Testamento de Sor Juana*, 21
94. Arenal and Powell, *Answer*, 5.
95. Ibid., 8.
96. Scott, *Madres del Verbo*, 61–88.
97. Arenal and Powell, *Answer*, 8.

1677 (*Songs of Praise for Pedro Nolasco*); *Neptuno Alegórico, 1680/1* (*Allegorical Neptune*); *Carta al pastor Antonio Nuñez de Miranda, 1681/2* (*Letter to the Reverend Nuñez de Miranda,* her confessor); *Primero Sueño, 1685–1688* (*First Dream*); *Soneta a Lysis, 1688* (*Sonnet to Lysis*); *Inundación Castálida, 1689* (*Fountain of the Muses*); *El Divino Narciso, 1690* (*The Divine Narcissus*); *Carta atenagórica, 1690* (*Letter Worthy of Athena*); *La Respuesta, 1691* (*The Answer*); and *Villancicos de Santa Catarina de Alejandría, 1691* (*Songs of Praise for St. Catherine of Alexandria*).

Sor Juana wrote a total of sixteen sets of *villancicos* for the Church.[98] Her most famous canticles were dedicated to St. Catherine of Alexandria, whom she revered, respected, and could relate to in terms of the similar struggles they shared as women in their lifetimes. They both were persecuted in their lifetimes. They both were challenged to renounce their faith and chose not to. Lastly, both were brought before an estimated fifty scholars in their lifetime to be questioned with regard to their intellect; in that context, both proved men wrong in their belief that women were incapable of engaging in intellectual discourse.

Sor Juana's *villancicos* were sung in the center of cultural life— in the cathedral of Puebla. They celebrate not only women but also protest patriarchal attitudes aimed at women. Two examples that Sor Juana wrote to celebrate St. Catherine of Alexandria clearly demonstrate this. The first is Poem 317, Carol VI.

> Catherine bears the victory!
> For with knowledge pure and holy
> She convinced the learned men
> And has emerged victorious
> —with her knowledge glorious—
> from their arrogance profane,
> which would convince and conquer her.
> But Catherine is the victor![99]

The second one is Poem 322, Carol XI.

98. Ibid., 17.
99. Ibid., 161.

Once upon a time this Girl,
as I say, was a very young thing,
just eighteen.
Hush now, be patient, and I'll explain.
And they say (how should I know
if it's true)
she knew a lot, although she was
just a girl.
Hush now, be patient,
and I'll tell you.
For, as we all know, they say

—*someone* says—

women can do nothing more
than spin and sew.
Hush now, be patient,
and you will know.
So: her arguments convinced
Mighty men!
(Any woman with a boy
easily wins.)
Hush now, be patient,
you'll hear it then.[100]

Sor Juana's final *villancico* was also dedicated to St. Catherine of Alexandria, the patroness of philosophers and young virgins.[101] Toward the end of Sor Juana's life I believe that her considerations of St. Catherine of Alexandria comforted her in the midst of crises in her life and her relationship with the Church. Here Sor Juana asserted, "She studies, and disputes, and teaches, thus she serves her Faith; for how could God, who gave her reason, want her ignorant. Victory! Victory!"[102]

Sor Juana died at three in the morning on Sunday April seventeenth of the year sixteen hundred and ninety five.[103] She was

100. Ibid., 169.

101. Paz, *Sor Juana*, 342.

102. Arenal and Powell, *Answer*, 161–163.

103. Cervantes, *Testamento de Sor Juana Inés de la Cruz*, 12.

forty-five years of age.[104] She died caring for her sick convent sisters.[105] In the year preceding Sor Juana's death, Mexico and her peoples were suffering as a result of widespread natural disasters and plagues.[106] Numerous individuals, *Mexicanos* (Mexicans) and not, lamented her death and the loss of a great literary figure, although the Church did not. Upon Sor Juana's death, the Church tried to erase her memory from history. Nevertheless, Sor Juana Inés de la Cruz is remembered in Spanish and Western history for her defense of women's rights, as well as her enormous output in the Golden Age of Spanish Literature. In a eulogy upon his friend's death, Don Carlos de Sigüenza y Góngora (1645–1700) said the following: [107]

> *No hay pluma alguna que su eminencia pueda levantar. Quisiera que fuera posible darle a ella la veneración que su trabajo merece para manifestar la naturaleza del conocimiento universal de su genio, para que nosotros en México podríamos apreciarla centenarios después de pasada la gracia y brillantez impartida a todas las mujeres aprendidas quienes son maravillas de la historia.*

> *There is no pen that can rise to her eminence. I wish that it were possible to give her the veneration that her work deserves, to make manifest the nature of the universal knowledge contained in her genius, so that we in Mexico could appreciate in centuries past the grace and brilliance imparted to all of those learned women who are marvels of history.*[108]

---

104. Paz, *Sor Juana*, 145.

105. Cervantes, *Testamento de Sor Juana Inés de la Cruz*, 12

106. Schons, "Obscure Points in the Life of Sor Juana," 57.

107. Castro Leal, *Poesia, Teatro y Prosa*, xiii.

108. Leonard, *Baroque Times in Old Mexico*, 191–192. The above quote is paraphrased and translated from Castilian Spanish.

SECTION II
Feminist Textual Analysis

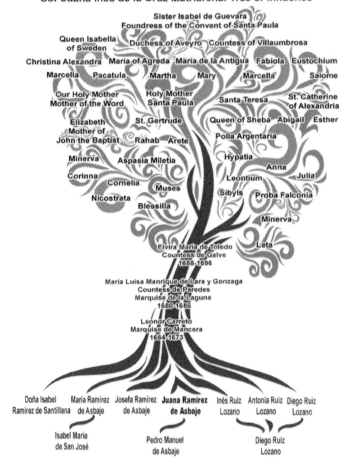

Sor Juana Inés de la Cruz Matriarchal Tree of Influence

CHAPTER 4

La Respuesta (The Answer)

Introduction

A PROLIFIC WRITER WHO worked in many genres, Sor Juana Inés de la Cruz wrote two works that specifically address the hardships that she endured throughout her life because of her gender, *El Sueño* and *La Respuesta*. In *La Respuesta*, she admits that, "I do confess that the trial[s] I have undergone [have] been beyond telling. For me, it has not been the knowledge (for I still know nothing) but the desire to know that has cost me so dear . . ."[1] *La Respuesta* is a response to a living nightmare, the nightmare that Sor Juana lived. Her world was dark, not light, dominated as it was by the Church and the Spanish Inquisition. The living nightmare that resulted came in an exchange of letters with the Jesuit theologian, Manuel Fernández de Santa Cruz (c.a. 1637–1699).[2] In that time, "letter writers understood that their letters would be read by more than just the addressee, even if they were not published," and that was exactly the intent.[3]

In 1690, Fernández de Santa Cruz, Jesuit and Bishop of Puebla, published two documents directed at Sor Juana and circulated

1. Arenal and Powell, *Answer*, 61.
2. Paz, *Sor Juana*, 398.
3. Kirk, *Sor Juana Inés de la Cruz*, 95.

them throughout Mexico.[4] The first was *Carta atenagórica* (*Letter Worthy of Athena*); the second, a theological treatise and attack on Sor Juana's critique of the well-known Portuguese Jesuit Antonio de Vieyra, who had argued that Christ's greatest *fineza* (demonstration of love) was His absence.[5] Sor Juana sharply disagreed and wrote that that the greatest *fineza* of Christ was not that "[H]e absented Himself from us," after His resurrection, but rather that He continued to be with God's people each and every time the Eucharist was celebrated.[6]

The arguments that Sor Juana makes in *La Respuesta*—her response to the letters of Fernández de Santa Cruz— foreshadow themes found in the work of twenty-first century Latina theologians: namely, that God continues to accompany God's people on a daily basis, in *la cotidiano*. Sor Juana believed that God desired to be in a reciprocal relationship with God's people.[7] In this way, her theological perspective affirmed the importance of free will in the life of the Christian believer.[8] At the same time, however, these interpretations threatened the Church's prescription for female behavior, since Sor Juana reclaimed the agency of all individuals, male and female, in their choice to engage, or not, in a relationship with God.[9] A connection of mutuality with the divine required freedom, and that meant freedom for everyone, not just men or Spaniards. This freedom suggested that women shared men's capacity for reasoning, a very problematic idea for clerics.[10] Hence *La Respuesta* is important in a number of respects.

4. Paz, *Sor Juana*, 389.

5. Ibid., 390–395.

6. Ibid., 392.

7. Ibid.

8. Ibid., 491.

9. Ibid., 395.

10. Arenal and Powell, *Answer*, 5

Summary and Historical Context

La Respuesta is one of two texts Sor Juana wrote to Jesuit clerics. The first, entitled *Autodefensa espiritual, Sor Juana*, was written in 1681.[11] It was never published. Rather, it was discovered in the early 1990s, nearly three hundred years after Sor Juana's death, by a Father Aureliano Tapia Méndez in a volume of archival documents that dated to eighteenth-century Mexico.[12] For Sorjuanista scholars, it is a landmark text because it reveals that the on-going conflict Sor Juana had with the Church neither began nor ended with *La Respuesta*.

Sor Juana's *Autodefensa Espiritual* was written exactly one decade before she wrote *La Respuesta* (1691). It was an angry letter to a cleric addressed to the Reverend Antonio Núñez de Miranda. The letter relieved him of his duty as Sor Juana's confessor.[13] Núñez de Miranda did not approve of Sor Juana's poetry, and he publicly chastised her.[14] In response, Sor Juana fired him.[15] Though nuns at the time had the option of changing confessors, most did not.[16] Thus, Sor Juana's choice was personal and political. She reclaimed her agency and right as a Christian woman to defend herself and her reputation against a misogynistic Jesuit cleric. In doing so, she also lambasted the larger institution that he represented, namely the Church and its Inquisition. In this text, one catches glimpses of Sor Juana's strength of character. Among the questions she raised were: "Why this attitude of making me out to be scandalous in front of everyone?"[17] "Why this discrediting of my person?"[18] "What wrong have I done to you to deserve your favor of speaking

---

11. Scott, *Madres del Verbo*, 61–82.

12. Paz, *Sor Juana*, 491.

13. Arenal and Powell, *Answer*, 8.

14. Ibid.

15. Ibid.

16. Ibid.

17. Scott, *Madres del Verbo*, 77.

18. Ibid.

so badly of me?"[19] "Am I perchance a heretic?"[20] She continues, "Then why is that, which in all others was considered good, judged to be evil in my case."[21] She concludes by mocking him and the Holy Office, asserting that he did not have the power to define her salvation in the next life. She declares that God alone has the right to judge her nature, writings, and spiritual practices.[22]

Like Núñez de Miranda, Fernández de Santa Cruz had known Sor Juana since her years in the viceregal court, but he had a long-standing positive relationship with her. Sor Juana was the half-sister of Inés Ruiz Lozano, the mother of Fray Miguel de Torres (fl. 16th cent.) who was Fernández de Santa Cruz's friend and biographer.[23] Thus, the nun belonged to a respectable family of clerics. Fernández de Santa Cruz seemed to recognize her literary talent and tolerated her because of her vocation, although he may have felt threatened by her too.

Unlike Núñez de Miranda, who publically berated Sor Juana in his own voice, Fernández de Santa Cruz wrote under a female pseudonym as *Sor Filotea de la Cruz*. Perhaps he was trying to diffuse or mask his attack on Sor Juana by situating it in the fabricated context of a dialogue between two nuns. In any case, he upbraided Sor Juana for spending too much time studying secular rather than sacred texts, deeming it a vain and presumptuous activity, inappropriate for a professed religious.[24] He criticized her transgressive behavior, declaring her subordinate in status to both men and to God. Fernández de Santa Cruz concluded Sor Filotea's letter by advising Sor Juana that it was in her best interest to change her ways by focusing on wisdom from above, in contrast to that which is "earthbound," or else she would go to "hell."[25] In other words, reading secular and scientific literature jeopardized her salvation.

19. Ibid.
20. Ibid.
21. Ibid., 76.
22. Ibid., 79.
23. Paz, *Sor Juana*, 67.
24. Trueblood, *Sor Juana Anthology*, 200.
25. Ibid.

In light of Sor Juana's previous disagreement with Núñez de Miranda, this threat undoubtedly angered her the most.

Why did Fernández de Santa Cruz, her long-time patron, censure Sor Juana in this way? He had expected to be elevated to the status of archbishop of Mexico, the highest position for a church official, and documents confirm that he was chosen to be successor to this rank.[26] Authorities in Madrid intervened, however, and the Jesuit Francisco Aguiar y Seijas (1632–1698) was appointed to this position instead.[27] Fernández de Santa Cruz took his revenge against the newly elected archbishop by using Sor Juana's criticism of Antonio de Vieyra (1608–1697)—a Jesuit philosopher whom Aquiar y Seijas respected and admired—against her.[28] Sor Juana's interpretation argued that freedom, or *libertad*, was necessary for a relationship with God. This reflected her shared value of the *libertad* for each and every person, especially for women. In the process, Sor Juana was treated like a pawn, "in [a] quarrel between two powerful Princes of the Roman Catholic Church."[29]

Comparing herself to St. Augustine, Mary, "Mother of the Word," Saul, and Moses, Sor Juana asserts in *La Respuesta*, that the charges rendered her speechless.[30] The timing of the *Carta atenagórica* was dire because at this point in her life Sor Juana lacked patrons who had the power and authority to stand up to the Church and the Spanish Inquisition. Though she had two nephews who were both clerics—the sons of her full sisters, Josefa and María—it was apparent that they did not have the clout to advocate on their aunt's behalf. From afar, the former viceroy and *virreina* back in Spain did their best to come to her defense, using their privilege, power, and influence, but distance made this challenging.[31] Like her nephews, her convent sisters also lacked the

26. Paz, *Sor Juana*, 402.

27. Ibid., 403.

28. Ibid.

29. Ibid.

30. Arenal and Powell, *Answer*, 39.

31. Paz, *Sor Juana*, 409.

leverage of the viceregal court since they lived under the direct jurisdiction of the Church.

For all intents and purposes Sor Juana was alone. I have no doubt that at the time Sor Juana was nervous about her relationship to both the Church and the Spanish Inquisition. Probably she had witnessed with her own eyes the agony of individuals brought before the Inquisition, tortured by fiendish devices, including *prensas* (presses), a reference she makes in *La Respuesta*.[32] Her exact words are, "how to render my thanks for the favor, as excessive as it was unexpected, of giving my drafts and scratches to the press; a favor so far beyond all measure as to surpass the most ambitious hopes or the most fantastic desires, so that as a rational being I simply could not house it in my thoughts."[33]

La Respuesta communicates a fear of "the Holy Office," which included the Church and Spanish Tribunal, the institutions responsible for the harrowing deaths of deviants like Sor Juana.[34] She would have known key individuals in this process, including the ecclesiastical judge and censor for the Holy Office, her former confessor, Núñez de Miranda.[35] Thus, a major purpose of *La Respuesta* is to announce that Sor Juana does not want any problems with the Church. It did not help that her former confessor had also publically undermined her character. All three of the clerics involved in the situation were Jesuits, a double threat because of the Jesuit role in supporting the Spanish Inquisition's agenda.

Sor Juana did not immediately respond to Sor Filotea's letter of condemnation. In the weeks after its publication it must have provoked suspicion among prelates in the Church and individuals in her familiar network. Each had an inside perspective on the political ramifications of this letter. Most may have known who published the letter and the rationale behind it. They may have wondered whether Sor Juana would respond to Sor Filotea's condemnation. *La Respuesta* illuminates how hurt she felt by her

32. Arenal and Powell, *Answer*, 39, 41.
33. Ibid.
34. Ibid., 47.
35. Paz, *Sor Juana*, 450.

mistreatment in general, but also by being betrayed by someone who once was a friend:

> And the most venomous and hurtful to me have not been those who with explicit hatred and ill-will have persecuted me, but those persons, loving me and desiring my good . . . who have mortified and tormented me more than any others.[36]

Sor Juana notes that that she wrote *La Respuesta* for three reasons. Her response echoed her rejoinder to Núñez de Miranda ten years earlier. First, she asserts a right to defend herself. Second, she decides to be true to her forthright, truthful nature.[37] More specifically, she states, "I confess with all the candor due to you and with the truth and frankness that are always at once natural and customary for me."[38] Lastly, she continues, "I had nearly resolved to leave the matter in silence; yet although silence explains much by the emphasis of leaving all unexplained, because it is a negative thing, one must name the silence, so that what it signifies may be understood. Failing that, silence will say nothing, for that is its proper function."[39]

Through her bluntness, Sor Juana shames Sor Filotea and all of the Jesuits who envied and resented her, not only for her nonconformity to prescribed norms for women, but also because her intellect surpassed theirs. We see evidence of this superior intellect in the vastness of her secular and religious references, not only to the Scriptures but also to Christian, Western, and Spanish history. Not only does Sor Juana argue that men do not recognize their own lack of talent, she asserts that this ignorance was the cause of Jesus' death.[40] His persecutors attacked Him, not only for doing, "good works," but also for the fame He received throughout

36. Arenal and Powell, *Answer*, 63.

37. Ibid., 45.

38. Ibid.

39. Ibid., 41, 43.

40. Ibid., 67.

the region, just as the Jesuits attacked Sor Juana for being so highly regarded.[41]

Sor Juana systematically refutes each condemnation made against her by Sor Filotea in *Carta atenagórica*. She repudiates the misogynistic and patriarchal assumptions that women are incapable of reason and are subordinate in status to men and God. She defends her passionate love of truth and her natural inclination to study as gifts from God.[42] Finally, Sor Juana declares that God alone has the power to judge her destiny and salvation when she declares:

> Blessed are you, my Lord God, for not only did you forbear to give another creature the power to judge me, nor have you placed that power in my hands. Rather, you have kept that power for yourself and have freed me of myself and of the sentence I would pass on myself, which, forced by my own conscience, could be no less than condemnation. Instead you have reserved that sentence for your great mercy to declare, because you love me more than I can love myself.[43]

Textual Analysis

La Respuesta is a public declaration of Sor Juana's desire to be a learned and educated woman.[44] Like clerics and peers in her time, she draws on resources in the Christian tradition such as Scripture, prominent authorities in Christianity, and select church doctrines to re-interpret and support her argument that women are as capable as men in engaging in theological discourse. The theme of *La Respuesta* is the misuse of knowledge. Sor Juana uses Sor Filotea's alias to her advantage: she plays along with the conceit

41. Ibid., 65.
42. Ibid., 49.
43. Ibid., 41.
44. Ibid., 49.

that she is merely having a discussion with another nun, and is thereby able to take some liberties in her response.

Sor Juana first responds to Sor Filotea's recommendation that she should spend more time studying sacred scriptures rather than profane texts and subjects. She then refutes and reinterprets Scriptures and church doctrines to argue that men and women are equal in their capacity to reason. Lastly, she creates a narrative in which her interpretation of Christ as beauty, and "head of Knowledge," shares characteristics with herself, as one also persecuted without a cause.[45] Unlike her male colleagues, Sor Juana integrates personal experiences of sexism and secondary resources, secular and religious, to support her claim that women are just as capable as men of reason and engaging in theological discourse. She avers, "Oh, how many abuses would be avoided in our land if the older women were well instructed."[46] Sor Juana's conclusion is that the world would be a more just place if women were educated.

Sor Juana's Defense

Sor Filotea's major prescription for Sor Juana is that she should focus more on "heavenly" than on "earth-bound knowledge."[47] Sor Filotea argues that individuals who study secular texts are more susceptible to vanity and vices. The exact words are, "It is a pity that so great a mind should stoop to lowly earthbound knowledge and not desire to probe into what transpires in heaven."[48] Sor Filotea does not stop there. "She" recognizes Sor Juana's, "keen mental powers," and, "clever mind," and continues saying that instead of, "exquisite favors, I consider them punishments."[49]

Sor Juana responds to this exhortation by saying: "my having written little on sacred matters has sprung from no dislike,

45. Ibid., 71.
46. Ibid., 85.
47. Trueblood, *Sor Juana Anthology*, 202.
48. Ibid.
49. Ibid.

nor from lack of application, but rather from a surfeit of awe and reverence toward those sacred letters, which I know myself to be so incapable of understanding and which I am so unworthy of handling."[50] She admits that there were times that she desired to study the sacred Scriptures but that she hesitated, realizing the repercussions that such a choice would have on her life and body by the Spanish Inquisition.[51] Her exact words are, "And thus I confess that often this very fear has snatched the pen from my hand and has made the subject matter retreat back toward that intellect from which it wished to flow; an impediment I did not stumble across with profane subjects, for a heresy against art is not punished by the Holy Office."[52] She continues by reminding Sor Filotea that some in her day insist it is not appropriate for a woman to study the Sacred Scriptures. Thus, "[H]ow should I dare take these [sacred scriptures] up in my unworthy hands, when sex and age and, above all, our customs oppose it?"[53]

Sor Juana is ingenious in her response: she demonstrates her knowledge of the Scriptures and defends her desire to read, write, and study them. She repeatedly denies that her writing has ever "proceeded from any dictate of my own but [rather] a force beyond me."[54] She proclaims that, "His Majesty knows why and to what end [God] did so."[55] "I have prayed that [God] snuff out the light of my intellect, leaving only enough to keep [God's] Law . . . [b]ut with regard to avoiding study absolutely, as such a thing does not lie within my power, I could not do it."[56] She declares,

> For ever since the light of reason first dawned in me, my inclination to letters was marked by such passion and vehemence that neither the reprimands of others (for I have received many) nor reflections of my own (there

50. Arenal and Powell, *Answer*, 45.

51. Ibid.

52. Ibid.

53. Ibid.

54. Ibid., 47.

55. Ibid.

56. Ibid.

have been more than a few) have sufficed to make me abandon my pursuit of this native impulse that God Himself bestowed on me.[57]

La Respuesta testifies that Sor Juana's talent has been both a blessing and curse. On the one hand, individuals in both the secular and religious spheres have recognized this talent and have asked her to write on certain subjects or themes. On the other hand, she has endured overwhelming persecution from others because of talents given to her by God. Sor Juana's perspective on knowledge differed from that of the Church. She argues that knowledge is not limited to books but rather includes "the intricate structures of this world," and all of God's creation.[58] In contrast to the Church, which argued that the Scriptures were uniquely the source of all wisdom, Sor Juana advocates different ways of knowing and knowledge, whether secular or religious, could be mediums for understanding the mysteries of the Christian faith. This is evident in her defense in which she integrates distinct figures in Christian, non-Christian, and even pagan traditions.

Re-Interpretation of Christian Doctrine

Sor Juana, like her male peers, draws on select church doctrines and historical figures in Christianity to understand classical interpretations of St. Paul's first letter to the Corinthians, that women should be silent in the churches (1 Cor 14:33b–36). She re-interprets this text to her advantage. First, Sor Juana states that all incompetent individuals, regardless of gender, should "remain silent."[59] She reasons that in order for individuals to fully learn, they must, "take heed . . . keep still," and listen, i.e., be silent.[60] She argues that this biblical passage addressed men and women equally. Her theological interpretation of this text is that the whole congregation, in-

57. Ibid.
58. Ibid., 73.
59. Ibid., 82.
60. Ibid., 89.

cluding men and women, were meant to be quiet.[61] In her view, St. Paul's call for women to be silent in the churches does not prohibit them from studying, reading, and writing, the activities for which she is being persecuted.[62]

Sor Juana continues saying that many women in the Christian tradition have been writers: so why should she be singled out for criticism, she asks. She further contends that all she has ever wanted to do through her studies was to become less ignorant.[63] She identifies and describes a world where women are the "good practitioners of knowledge."[64] Thus, Sor Juana begins by situating herself within a long lineage of Roman Catholic men and women who have used knowledge for the benefit of the Church. With this goal in mind she reclaims her agency as a Christian woman by self-identifying as the daughter of Saint Jerome and Santa Paula protesting that, "It would be degeneracy for an idiot daughter to proceed from such learned parents."[65]

Sor Juana then addresses the use and misuse of knowledge, noting that neither sex is exempt from abusive practices.[66] She refers to these individuals as "bad practitioners" of knowledge who she feels debase verses, "fashioning devil's snares of them."[67] Sor Juana identifies individuals in the past and present, men and women, who used their knowledge well, including her spiritual father, St. Jerome (347–420), Juan Díaz de Arce (1594–1653), Lupercio Leonardo (1559–1613), Santa Paula, Santa Teresa, and St. Catherine of Alexandria (282–305).[68] Sor Juana also mentions men who misused knowledge, resulting in harm, "like putting a sword in the hands of a madman."[69] Among the men she singles

61. Ibid., 77.
62. Ibid., 91.
63. Ibid., 47.
64. Ibid., 95.
65. Ibid., 53.
66. Ibid., 95.
67. Ibid.
68. Ibid., 75, 79.
69. Ibid., 85.

out are the "wicked Pelagius," the "perverse Arius," the "wicked Luther," and "all other heretics like our own Dr. Cazalla" (fl. 16th century), a medical doctor in her region who she adds, "was neither our own, nor our doctor."[70]

Sor Juana disputes Sor Filotea's argument that women are incapable of reason when she presents a long line of Christian and Gentile women who used their knowledge and education in positive ways for the advancement of their peoples. In her litany she includes women in Christian and Western history who "merited titles."[71] Not only does she recognize a "vast throng" of women in secular and religious domains, she also situates these women's use of knowledge as equal to or surpassing male knowledge and leadership.[72] In this way, she presents an alternative to that of the dominant Western history, which, for the most part, focuses exclusively on men. Sor Juana begins her catalog by celebrating Deborah, one of the Israelite judges, for exercising military and political leadership, while at the same time "governing the people among whom there were many learned men."[73] She remembers the legacy of the Queen of Sheba who used her knowledge exceedingly well and "dared to test the wisdom of the wisest of men with riddles, without being rebuked for it."[74] Sor Juana adds that it was on this account that she was a judge to unbelievers. She also highlights Abigail, "for the gift of prophecy," Rahab, for "piety," and Anna who possessed the gift of "perseverance."[75]

Among the women whom Sor Juana integrates into her listing of non-Christian women were the Sibyls whom she states were chosen by God to prophesize the essential mysteries of the Faith.[76] She includes Minerva, the daughter of great Jupiter who was

70. Ibid., 83.
71. Ibid., 79.
72. Ibid.
73. Ibid., 77.
74. Ibid.
75. Ibid.
76. Ibid.

adored in her time as the goddess of the sciences.[77] She recounts the legacy of Zenobia, "queen of the Palmyrians," who was recognized for her wisdom and courage, and Aspasia Miletia, professor in the disciplines of philosophy and rhetoric and teacher to the great legislator Pericles.[78] She also names Nicostrata, remembered for her mastery of Latin and Greek wisdom.[79] She concludes by reclaiming the legacies of Hypatia, who "taught astronomy and lectured for many years in Alexandria," and Leontium, who "won over the philosopher Theophrastus and proved him wrong."[80] Sor Juana's decision to reclaim pagan women as mediums of knowledge and teachers in the Christian faith must have irritated the clerics reading this impressive list.

Persecuted Without a Cause: Jesus and Sor Juana

Sor Juana also examines men's relationship to Jesus. She condemns patriarchal assumptions that have been used to privilege men over women before God. She refutes the concept that men are equal in power to God because they share the same sex. *La Respuesta* focuses on Christian behaviors in contrast to abstract ideologies. Sor Juana states that the men who witnessed Jesus being crucified were "crude" and "base."[81] They, His opponents argued that He was "a transgressor against the law, a trouble maker who with His deceits stirs up the people."[82] Sor Juana writes that these men lied when they said this about Jesus, and concludes that in her experience the "learned sex, [i.e., men] . . . fall[s] prey to passion," and thus "burst[s] out illogically in just this fashion."[83]

Sor Juana asks how could these individuals not love Jesus for the many miracles He performed. He made the sick healthy,

77. Ibid., 79.
78. Ibid.
79. Ibid.
80. Ibid.
81. Ibid., 65.
82. Ibid.
83. Ibid.

revived the dead, and cast out devils from those possessed. Paradoxically, "it was for this very reason that they did not love Him."[84] Rather, "they despised Him!"[85] They—that is, men—took His life.[86] In response Sor Juana declares, "May God preserve me if working miracles is cause that one should die!"[87] Implicitly, Sor Juana makes parallels between herself and Jesus for being deemed significant and doing good works.[88] For this, they both were scorned.

Sor Juana continues her argument by differentiating the kinds of crowns given in the first century.[89] In Jesus' time, the civic crown was given to those "who saved the life of a fellow citizen."[90] The mural crown was given to individuals who "scaled walls."[91] Sor Juana asserts that of all the crowns conferred on individuals the greatest one was bestowed on Jesus, the *obsidio* crown.[92] She argues that this crown was appropriate for Jesus because of the etymology of the word, *obsidio*, which means siege.[93] It was given to an individual who freed, or liberated, a besieged city.[94] Like Jesus, Sor Juana sought to liberate the people of her own era from the bondage of the Church and Spanish Crown. With this example in mind, she says that the "Head that is a treasure of wisdom can hope for nothing more than thorns,"[95] a reference to the crown of thorns. She feels that Jesus died because of men's, not women's, envious nature.

Sor Filotea's words in *Carta atenagórica* must have echoed in Sor Juana's mind, berating her by saying, "All this studying is not

84. Ibid.
85. Ibid.
86. Ibid., 67.
87. Ibid., 65.
88. Ibid., 67.
89. Ibid.
90. Ibid., 69.
91. Ibid.
92. Ibid.
93. Ibid.
94. Ibid.
95. Ibid.

fitting, for holy ignorance is your duty; she shall go to perdition, she shall surely be cast down from such heights by that same wit and cleverness."[96] Sor Juana asks, "How [am] I to bear up against this? A strange martyrdom indeed, where I must be both martyr and my own executioner!"[97] She testifies to the persecution she endured by individuals who envied and resented her. Like Jesus, Sor Juana was persecuted as an innocent person.

Conclusion

Sor Juana argues that the world would be a more just place if women were educated. She states, "Oh, how many abuses could be avoided in this land if only the women were as well instructed."[98] Her litany of names supports her argument that women are just as capable, as men, and often more so, in engaging in the domain of reason. Her personal experiences of abuse and abandonment led her to outline some parameters with regard to the education of women. She was acutely aware that women, particularly young maidens, were susceptible to physical violation by men. Thus, she argues that men and women should be taught in different educational settings in order to avoid, "considerable harm," to women.[99]

Sor Juana's theological perspective, informed by experience and scientific inquiry, led her to conclude that men and women were equal in their capacity to lead and engage in intellectual discourse. Her mother exemplified the ability of women to take on leadership positions that required financial competence, managerial and entrepreneurial skills. Doña Isabel Ramírez had maintained a hacienda and thus relationships with the Church and local business owners. As a young adult, Sor Juana was exposed to still more competent women in the viceregal court. It was there that Sor Juana was encouraged to apply her talents and gifts. She learned Latin, and this opened her mind to Christian doctrines in

96. Trueblood, *Sor Juana Anthology*, 200.
97. Arenal and Powell, *Answer*, 63.
98. Ibid., 85.
99. Ibid., 65.

the West, through the study of theology, philosophy, and Sacred Scriptures, primarily the Vulgate as translated in the fourth century by the patron of her convent, Saint Jerome.

Sor Juana was exposed to competent and skilled women who ran her convent like a modern-day corporation.[100] Contrary to stereotypes of convent life these institutions played significant roles in the economy of the European Middle Ages and seventeenth-century New Spain. Though their primary role was to provide charity to the poor and education for children, convents also participated in the market-economy of their times.[101] In Sor Juana's day convents were autonomous institutions, free of church intervention with regards to financial affairs.[102] Because Sor Juana was an entrepreneur like her mother, her convent sisters nominated her to be what today is called the financial officer. She oversaw the convent's expenditures and revenues, property investments, and the dowries collected from entering novices. She may have even played a formative role as head mistress of entering novices.

Sor Juana's evolving assessment of male-dominated systems began with experiential wisdom. The reality was that in her time women were not encouraged to pursue higher levels of education. In *La Respuesta*, she asserts that this was one of the challenges she experienced: not to have peers or a teacher with whom to test out her ideas and hypotheses.[103] She only had what she called mute books.[104] Thus in all three stages of her life, scientific inquiries were based on her personal experiences, from her early girlhood observations of the separation of the egg and yolk, to her observations of how men treated women in the court, to life in the convent when, denied access to study, she pondered the lines of the wood at the top of the refectory to discern if the lines were parallel.[105] Thus her life and work have implications for Latina feminist theologians today.

100. Paz, *Sor Juana*, 119.

101. Ibid.

102. Ibid., 118, 121.

103. Arenal and Powell, *Answer*, 53.

104. Ibid.

105. Ibid., 51.

CHAPTER 5

El Sueño (The Dream)

Introduction

IN THE PREVIOUS CHAPTERS I explored my hypothesis that various communities of women with whom Sor Juana Inés de la Cruz was affiliated informed her attitudes and critiques of prescribed gender norms. I argued that these women nurtured Sor Juana's critical view of patriarchy in her seventeenth-century New Spain world between men and women, as well as between Spaniards and non-Spaniards. In this chapter I continue to analyze these themes in Sor Juana's primary document, *El Sueño*. I chose this text as well as *La Respuesta* because in Sor Juana's vast oeuvre of writings they were written in the first person rather than the third. I think these texts complement each other; one is personal, the other is public, and thus more overtly political. Considered together, they provide a more complex glimpse of Sor Juana's public and private personas.

In Spanish, the term *sueño* has multiple definitions. Literally, it means sleep.[1] It is also used to describe a person's state of being, personal ambitions and dreams in life.[2] In Sor Juana's *sueño*, all three definitions overlap in her-story of a non-gendered soul that moves through liminal spaces and time envisioning a world where all souls, male and female, Spanish and non-Spanish, are liberated. In contrast to Aristotelian, Platonic and subsequently Christian thought—that argued that an individual's soul or body

1. Paz, *Sor Juana*, 360.
2. Ibid.

was gendered dictated by hierarchical dualisms that elevated man over women, mind over body, and soul over spirit—Sor Juana reinterprets these oppressive interpretations to her advantage emphasizing the opposite, a liberated non-gendered soul.

In *La Respuesta*, Sor Juana says that *El Sueño* was the only text that she wrote for her own pleasure, and dismisses it, saying that it was a trifle of a text.[3] Yet *El Sueño* is her most intimate work, which came from her heart rather than at the behest of religious or political authorities. In Spain, it was considered a literary masterpiece whereas in her native land it generated further animosity between her and clerics who were envious of the recognition and admiration she was receiving in both hemispheres.[4] Like Jesus, she was not seen as a leader by her home town.

The precise date *El Sueño* was composed is unknown. Paz proposes that it was written in 1685, yet I find no evidence to substantiate this claim.[5] Undeniably it was written prior to 1692 when Sor Juana's patroness, María Luisa, Marquise of Mancera, published it in a second volume of the nun's writings in Spain entitled *Obras Completas* or *Complete Works*.[6] I propose that *El Sueño* was written in 1688 or 1689, shortly after her mother Doña Isabel Ramírez died in 1688 and her dear companion and patroness the *virreina*, María Luisa, left for Spain that same year.[7]

Sor Juana wrote many documents to celebrate historic moments and loss of significant figures in New Spain's history. Between 1676 and 1679, she wrote five *villancicos* to celebrate the Immaculate Conception, the Feast of the Assumption and the birthdays of King Charles II and Don Pedro Velázquez de la Cadena, her sponsor to enter the convent of Santa Paula.[8] Between 1681 and 1689, Sor Juana wrote at least ten *villancicos*. The majority

---

3. Arenal and Powell, *Answer*, 97.

4. Paz, *Sor Juana*, 357.

5. Ibid., 356.

6. Ibid.

7. Ibid., 67, 266.

8. Ibid., 137. Trueblood, *Sor Juana*, 123–124; 127–129.

were for the Virgin Mary whom she refers to as "Our Lady," queen, or *virreina*, of Heaven.[9]

This time the losses were personal. I imagine how distressed Sor Juana was at this point in time. Though I assume that her full-sisters Josefa and María did support her, they could not be physically present to her in the convent. However, María's daughter, Sister Isabel María de San José, could, and I envision Isabel at her Aunt Juana's side during this trying period in her life. Sor Juana was a strong woman, but it is difficult to be strong all the time. I see Isabel affirming her dear aunt and patroness saying, *querida Tia, estarás bien* (My dear aunt, you will be well). *Calmate su mente y cuerpo* (Calm down your mind and body). I imagine Isabel mopping her grieving Aunt Juana's brow with a cloth. Sor Juana did indeed lie down and rest her body and mind.

I suggest it was in this context that Sor Juana's literary dream took form, quite possibly in response to the loss of these two women, so important as mentors and models. Sor Juana, in desperate need of comfort, gave birth to her most profound and intimate poem in the silence of her private cell and library. On one particular such night, I think Sor Juana befriended the creative imagination of her youth. I suspect Sor Juana wrote the poem for herself, not necessarily for others: not only to console herself but also to reaffirm that God alone—neither men nor institutions—had the ultimate authority to pass judgment on her salvation. In her own words she states,

> And so when I consider this fully, here in solitude, it is my custom to say: Blessed are you, my Lord God, for not only did you forbear to give another creature the power to judge me, nor have you placed that power in my hands. Rather, you have kept that power for yourself and have freed me of myself and of the sentence I would pass on myself, which, forced by my own conscience could be no less than condemnation. Instead you have reserved

9. Trueblood, *Sor Juana*, 130–137.

that sentence for your great mercy to declare, because
you love me more than I can love myself.[10]

Methodology

To analyze Sor Juana's dream three centuries removed from her
New Spain world is a daunting task. For me, Sor Juana's *El Sueño* is
so complex that no one except she can fully understand the layers
of meaning that weaves her-story dream-plot together. Recognizing this, for this analysis, I will examine Sor Juana's nine hundred
and seventy-five-line poem in three sections.[11] I will employ a close
reading and feminist literary analysis of the terms "silence" and
"noise." I hypothesize each section reflects one stage of Sor Juana's
her-story. I argue that for Sor Juana silence reflects the harmony of
God's reign, while noise is the antithesis.

Textual Analysis

Sor Juana's *El Sueño* seems to be an extension of the three matriarchal communities of women that shaped her evolving critiques
of inequalities in her seventeenth-century New Spain world. I
propose this analysis recognizing that Sor Juana's dream, like the
three stages of her life, were matricentric. It is a world, or rather a
cosmos, where women reign. Similar to her youth, in her young
and mature adult years Sor Juana is surrounded by prominent
and powerful women figures in ancient civilizations including the
Greeks and Romans, Nahuas and Christians. *El Sueño* is a prototypical feminist and ecofeminist dream where women are role
models of what a more just world looks like.

Sor Juana's dream is a meta- and mega-epic narrative of
shared experiences of discrimination that she and other women
and non-Spaniards in New Spain experienced in their lifetimes. It
is a her and their-story narrative that seeks reconciliation between

10. Arenal and Powell, *Answer*, 41.
11. Paz, *Sor Juana*, 367–368.

Christian Iberian Spaniards, non-Spaniards and a newly emerging Christian *criollo* and *mestizo* New Spain population. In *El Sueño*, Sor Juana's underlying argument is that the two dominant civilizations in her region, Spanish and non-Spanish, both reflect God's beauty, and thus are equally a part of Christian salvation history. Her dream testifies to the challenges imposed upon an oppressed majority by an elite minority, namely the Church and Spanish Inquisition. In this journey of the soul, Sor Juana moves in between spaces of noise and silence. For the poet, "noise" and "silence" are personal and collective: personal in that silence is the medium for her to connect with the God whom she worships in prayer, and collective in that for her *silencio*, silence signifies harmony in her universe. Noise interrupts this harmony.

Sor Juana—like the Nahua people and European authors such as Chaucer, Spenser, Shakespeare, and Milton—utilized myths to explore the epistemological question of humanity's relationship to nature, human beings, God, and the cosmos.[12] Edith Hamilton, in *Mythology: Timeless Tales of Gods and Heroes*, asserts that classical Greek and Roman mythologies historically have been used for two purposes. First, they have been "a point of departure" to examine contemporary problems of specific time periods.[13] Second, they have been a resource to, "retrace the path from [a] civilized [humanity] who lives so far from nature," to a humanity, "who live[s] in close companionship with nature."[14] Sor Juana's dream does exactly that.

Sor Juana's point of departure is a pre-Columbian Mesoamerican worldview in which the cosmos revolves around *Naturaleza* (Nature), the *sol* (sun), the *luna* (moon), and the *estrellas* (stars). In contrast to the Spanish worldview, which emphasized the superiority of humans over nature, and Europeans over indigenous peoples, Sor Juana's *sueño* reclaims the cosmic worldview of her people, the Nahua population. It is a geocentric cultural universe that reflects Nahua principles of complementarity between gods

12. León-Portilla, *Aztec Thought and Culture*, 1. Hamilton, *Mythology*, 10.

13. Ibid., 10.

14. Ibid.

and goddesses, males and females, and human and non-human nature.[15] In this way, Sor Juana connects the epic narratives of Roman and Greek *historiadores* (historians), such as *Homero* (Homer), to a Nahua Aztec Mesoamerican worldview where the primal value of their civilization was a communal and ecological sensitivity to the earth and its regenerative capacity.[16]

Like her antecedents, Sor Juana uses mythic figures from the Greek and Roman (European), and Nahua (Mesoamerican) traditions to create her personal her-story narrative and that of her people. It is a cosmic plot that tells a story of injustice in Spanish America. In this universe, Sor Juana is the heroine, taking a journey as a non-gendered soul in a noisy, patriarchal world. But she is not alone. Her "audacious" and "daring sisters," goddesses and heroines, will be her patronesses and guides.[17] They are her foremothers, living and dead, mythical and metaphorical. Like them, Sor Juana will push on *con tardo vuelo y canto* (in flight and song) to the *Cielo* (Heavens) though possibly in *vanos* (vain).[18]

The social structure in Sor Juana's poem is egalitarian: Men and women and gods and goddesses are notably equal protagonists in her-story poem. In her dream they are the Roman gods and goddesses, Diana, Jupiter and Venus while the Greek gods and goddesses are the daughters of Minya, Dionysus, Pluto, and Atalanta. While *El Sueño* has major and minor characters, nonetheless each character with his or her qualities, attributes, strengths, and weaknesses, plays a role.

Like feminists today, Sor Juana begins her narrative by situating her her-story within her social location. She does not name the origin of the conflicts in her region, but through descriptive adjectives she narrates the history of the Nahua people that resulted from the encounter between Mesoamerica and Spain. In her dream, the people of her region are "mocked *from afar.*"[19] Ill

---

15. Marcos, "Mesoamerican Religions," 654–655.

16. Sayers Peden, *Sor Juana Inés de la Cruz,* 98.

17. Ibid., 81.

18. Ibid., 79.

19. Ibid.

omens attest to *funesta[s]* (pending disaster) in the region. Though not named, in Nahua history, Montezuma, the ancient Aztec leader had an ill omen prior to the arrival of Spaniards and the demise of Tenochtitlan.[20] In a similar way, the ill-omen Sor Juana alludes to in her poem signifies noise, or outside force, entering the region. Prior to the conquest and Spanish rule on the continent there was an *imperioso silencio* (silent empire).[21] Sor Juana's world was harmonious and in balance. Now her world and cosmos were marked by extreme contrasts of silence and noise, light and darkness. Characteristic of New Spain's beauty, (*Las*) *Pyramidales*, (Pyramids) are surrounded by *sombras* (shadows) evoking fear in native persons.[22] Soon, the land and its women would be violated by *sacrílego rüido* (sacrilegious noise).[23]

In Sor Juana's her-story, she is a non-gendered soul in flight looking over her Pre-Hispanic and New Spain world. In Nahua thought, she is the *tonalli* that travels at night during dreams.[24] In the Christian tradition she is on a journey often referred to as a pilgrimage.[25] In Sor Juana's dream the light from the Roman goddess of the moon, Diana, makes it possible for her to see remnants of the glorious and ancient legacy of the Nahua people prior to the conquest: its pyramids, convexes, and obelisks. Sor Juana is filled with terror at what she sees: mass destruction. Forces from outside her social location's boundaries violate space and time, oppressing her and her people. Darkness permeates the land that evokes dread by external forces: "gaseous blackness," "dread," "shade," "defilement," and a "shadowy war."[26] *El aire* (the air) is *denso* (dense).[27] The land has been "conquered."[28] It is difficult for Sor Juana to

---

20. Schwartz, *Victors and Vanquished*, 29–31.

21. Sayers Peden, *Sor Juana Inés de la Cruz*, 78–79.

22. Ibid.

23. Ibid., 82.

24. Marcos, *Taken From The Lips*, 6.

25. Paz, *Sor Juana*, 360.

26. Sayers Peden, *Sor Juana Inés de la Cruz*, 79.

27. Ibid.

28. Ibid.

respirar (breathe).[29] Still, Diana's light outshines the darkness and Sor Juana continues to move, "heaven[ward]" and sees the glorious pyramids, over and against "muted voices" and "silence."[30]

In the first stage of Sor Juana's life and journey the primary female figures are the great Goddess Diana, the dishonored child Nyctímene, and the daughters of Minyas who were disobedient to male-authority, in this case, the Roman god, Baco, or Bacchus. In Sor Juana's narrative, the goddess Diana is the central figure. She is *la protectora* (protectoress) of this *imperio* (empire).[31] She maintains harmony and balance in the region. She has many titles that appeal to Sor Juana. She is the patroness of unmarried girls and of chastity.[32] She is the goddess "of the vegetative life," and is "not under the care of man."[33] Most importantly, she is the goddess where three crossroads meet.[34] In Sor Juana's world, I think these crossroads symbolize the three primary cultures of her era, which included the native population, black Africans and Spaniards, born both in the Americas and the Iberian Peninsula. Geographically, Sor Juana's world also had three canals that connected individuals in her region: Iztapalapa, Tepeaquilla, and Chapultepec.[35] For Sor Juana, these were important metaphors because they reflected her desire for unity between these three cultures.

In New Spain, the goddess Diana had a similar leadership role to that of the ancient Aztec Great Goddess, Coyolxauhqui, who resided in the Pyramid of the Moon.[36] In Mesoamerican thought, Coyolxauhqui, was Mother Earth. Like the great goddess Diana, Coyolxauhqui was associated with the moon. Similarly, both were guardians of life and of the regenerative capacity of the earth.[37]

29. Ibid.
30. Ibid.
31. Ibid.
32. Howe and Herrer, *Handbook of Classical Mythology,* 81.
33. Ibid.
34. Ibid.
35. León-Portilla, *The Broken Spears,* xvii.
36. Miller, *The Art of Mesoamerica,* 69.
37. Ibid.

Most importantly, like Diana, Coyolxauhqui's supernatural forces permeated the region maintaining harmony and balance. In Sor Juana's world, I suspect that under the dual-leadership of Coyolxauhqui and Diana's *el silencio no se interumpia* (silence was not interrupted).[38] It is possible that Sor Juana considered herself not only the temporal or biological daughter of Doña Isabel Ramírez but also the spiritual and eternal daughter of these otherworldly goddesses, since her illegitimacy was problematic.

In the following section and stage of Sor Juana's poem, the Roman god Baco, more commonly known as Bacchus or Dionysus in classical Greek mythology enters the story.[39] In *El Sueño* Baco pressures the three daughters of Minya to serve him.[40] They disobey his orders, instead continuing to weave, sew, and attend to other household tasks.[41] To chastise them, he turns them into bats.[42] They were *castigado tremendo* (dreadfully punished).[43] Baco made the layers of their skin so thin that they were vulnerable to the elements.[44] I suspect for Sor Juana, the wings might symbolize the laws that appeared to protect women, but in reality hindered their flight.

Sor Juana depicts Baco as being "mad,"[45] in contrast to the daughters of Minya. She attributes this characteristic, normally associated with women, to this male mythic character. It is one of many gender twists in Sor Juana's *sueño* that presents a more egalitarian world between the sexes. I think that the daughters of Minya harkin her back to the first stage of her life on the haciendas of Sor Juana's birth and youth where numerous women, including her mother, her full- and stepsisters, and her grandmother surrounded her; women who, like Sor Juana, were undoubtedly

38. Sayers Peden, *Sor Juana Inés de la Cruz*, 78.

39. Hamilton, *Mythology*, 54–62.

40. Sayers Peden, *Sor Juana Inés de la Cruz*, 39, 81.

41. Ibid.

42. Ibid.

43. Ibid., 49, 80.

44. Ibid., 50–51.

45. Ibid., 80.

more interested in reading, writing, and sewing than heeding to the dictates of men.

The next mythic figure in Sor Juana's her-story narrative is the Roman goddess Nyctímene.[46] In George Howe and G.A. Herrer's *Handbook of Classical Mythology*, Nyctímene dishonored her family by committing incest with her father without his knowledge.[47] In Sor Juana's her-story the Roman goddess Minerva takes pity on Nyctímene as she was hiding with shame.[48] Subsequently, Minerva changed Nyctímene into an owl, a sacred animal associated with this deity.[49] I suspect Nyctímene's mythic story speaks to Sor Juana's her-story in multiple ways. First, it reflects Sor Juana's experience as a young girl and a young adult who was blessed to be surrounded by the support and protection of women. Minerva, along with Sor Juana's mother, grandmother, and the *virreinas*, took Sor Juana under their wings, and became the patroness to her protégée. Second, Sor Juana, like Nyctímene, brought dishonor to her family for her status as a child born out of wedlock. She was also a disgrace for essentially being herself, a somewhat deviant child. She did not accept the social norms of her times regarding women's behavior. From the standpoint of many around her she engaged in "sacrilegious" behaviors.[50] Unlike other girls her age, Sor Juana enjoyed *confabulaciónes* or "schemes," of her own making.[51]

Sor Juana becomes Minerva's apprentice in her-story poem. In gratitude to her patroness, who had metaphorically saved her life from her father's wrath, Sor Juana in return wants to safeguard the holy oil the Church used that was pressed from the roots of Minerva's tree.[52] In Sor Juana's narrative she breaks into the Church hiding at the highest point of the church, the clerestory, and waits

46. Ibid.
47. Howe and Herrer, *Handbook of Classical Mythology*, 180.
48. Sayers Peden, *Sor Juana Inés de la Cruz*, 81.
49. Howe and Herrer, *Handbook of Classical Mythology*, 180.
50. Sayers Peden, *Sor Juana Inés de la Cruz*, 79, 83.
51. Ibid.
52. Ibid., 81.

for the right time to "draw near" to the "holy lamps."[53] Her intention is to get close enough to the "eternal flames" of the church to
extinguish them, salvaging Minerva's precious oil.[54] In Sor Juana's
time it was a sacrilegious act for a woman because she crossed a
boundary for women in the Church by getting near to God's taber-
nacle where the flame resided. As a young girl, Sor Juana felt protected by Minerva's wisdom and knowledge, and this may explain
why she felt connected to this goddess who was patroness of both
wisdom and, "persons engaged in the learned professions."[55] This
is why I think Sor Juana refused to give up the "holy lamp" and
"oil" of this patroness.

Next, Sor Juana's her-story focuses on the Greek god Dionysus. I think Dionysus reflects the first and second stage of Sor Juana's
life. Like the Roman goddess Diana, the Greek god Dionysus has
multiple titles and symbols associated with him. In Greek mythology he is referred to by many names, including Lyaeus, Bromius,
Evius, Iacchus, Zagreus, and Thyoneus.[56] In Roman mythology, his
name is Liber, "the son of Zeus and Semele, or Thyone."[57] In classical mythology, Dionysus is one of "two great Gods of Earth." [58]
The latter is Demeter, the Goddess of Wine.[59] Together, they were
considered "mankind's best friends."[60]

In his story, Dionysus, like Sor Juana, invites God's people
to worship God "everywhere on earth."[61] He travelled widely
to share the good news of all gods. Along the way he had a
revelation that all cultures and peoples were distinct and valu-
able. I suspect that for Sor Juana, Dionysus was a perfect role
model of an individual who respects difference, diverse cultures,

53. Ibid., 79.
54. Ibid.
55. Howe and Herrer, *Handbook of Classical Mythology*, 83.
56. Ibid.
57. Ibid.
58. Hamilton, *Mythology*, 47.
59. Ibid.
60. Ibid.
61. Ibid.

civilizations, and peoples.[62] Similarly, Sor Juana also had a celebratory attitude toward diversity represented across civilizations. These values resonate with her exposure to the gods and goddesses in the Nahua tradition that continued to grow in Sor Juana's thought processes as a young adult. Moreover, Dionysus was also concerned about the well being of all members of society.[63] In Sor Juana's time this concern could reflect a respect for all individuals regardless of a person's sex, race, class, ethnic background, religious affiliation and most probably sexual affiliation.[64]

Sor Juana, like Dionysus, used the written word in songs, *villancicos*, prayers, Marian devotions to share the good news of the gospel. Her drama, *El Divino Narciso*, is one example of this. In this play she highlights similarities between a Spanish and Mesoamerican understanding of God who is the origin of life and death and calls believers to worship Him/Her. Like Dionysus, Sor Juana was a seeker, sojourner and individual who valued the wisdom of ancient civilizations. Distinctive to Sor Juana's her-story is that she, like Dionysus, valued the ecological and regenerative capacities of the earth.

The Roman god Pluto appears next in Sor Juana's herstory.[65] He is the antithesis of Dionysus. He is the "loose-tongued minister."[66] Unlike the Nahua people, Pluto sings, *a capella,* without accompaniment.[67] He tries to orchestrate a choir but is not successful. It was not "awe-inspiring," "summoning [one] to wakefulness," but rather "persuaded one to sleep."[68] It had no harmony, rhyme, or reason in it. As a result, people declined to listen to anything he sang. For Sor Juana it was noise. She describes it as "appalling," "tuneless," and "apathetic."[69] She continues, saying

62. Ibid., 148.

63. Howe and Herrer, *Handbook of Classical Mythology*, 83.

64. Ibid.

65. Sayers Peden, *Sor Juana Inés de la Cruz*, 70.

66. Ibid., 81.

67. Ibid.

68. Ibid.

69. Ibid.

it was *tan detenido* (so lethargic) that even the wind fell asleep out of boredom.[70] In Sor Juana's poem, Pluto epitomizes disharmony in the region through his resistance to diverse voices and peoples. In this god there is neither harmony, nor silence and thus God is not present.

In Sor Juana's her-story narrative, Pluto was solely interested in hearing his own voice. It is quite likely that Pluto represents the Church, which in Sor Juana's time was resistant to marginal voices, including women and non-Spaniards. The Church was not interested in collaboration and so church authorities were not models of harmony. In her era the Church had an authoritative voice but for her and her peoples it was just noise. Perhaps Sor Juana thought that if they would only listen to the songs, dances and wisdom of the Nahua people, then Iberian Spaniards and creoles, as well as the Church, could learn something. In contrast to the goddess Diana, who brings harmony to the region, Pluto's presence and music is noisy, maybe even sacrilegious as well.

In the third stage of Sor Juana's life, the Greek goddess Atalanta figures prominently, symbolic of the internal freedom she felt as an independent intellectual.[71] Atalanta, like Sor Juana, had no interest in marriage.[72] Rather, each enjoyed their lives as a free and liberated woman. Although Atalanta, had many suitors, neither she nor Sor Juana were interested in being in a marital relationship with a man, particularly not with one who was not her intellectual equal.[73] In all three stages of her life, Sor Juana did not have significant strong male figures. Rather it was her mother, sisters, grandmother and the *virreinas* who were there for her. Because it was nearly impossible to be in an egalitarian relationship with the opposite sex in the seventeenth century, Sor Juana chose life in the convent as an alternative to marriage. There she, like so many women in her time, had the freedom to be true to herself, and her

---

70. Ibid., 80–81.

71. Zimmerman, *Dictionary of Classical Mythology*, 35.

72. Ibid.

73. Ibid.

sex, while at the same time protecting herself from what she calls in *La Respuesta* crude and violent men.[74]

Sor Juana's her-story concludes with the Roman goddess of love, Venus. For Sor Juana, Venus would bridge the east (Spain) and the west (New Spain) together in harmony.[75] She is also the brightest star to shine over the whole universe or cosmos.[76] In this harmonious world, Huitzilopochtli, the Aztec sun god, and Jesus, the Son of God would equally be respected for the ancient wisdom that each held in their respective traditions.[77] At the end of Sor Juana's dream she wakes up surrounded by light, presumably that of Venus.[78] I suggest that this light, for Sor Juana, indicates the possibility of an authentic and real harmony in her social location, particularly between Spaniards and non-Spaniards. Sor Juana did not see this dream actualized in her lifetime. Still, her hope for reconciliation between these two highly sophisticated civilizations continues in U.S. Latina Theology today.

Conclusion

Sor Juana's *sueño* lays the foundation for a Christian anthropology that recognized both New Spain and Spain as ancient and noble civilizations. For her, a civilized nation and world was where people of different ethnic backgrounds, races, religious preferences, and sexes were equally valued. It ponders the tensions that co-existed in her land while at the same time envisioning a renewed society where all relationships between humans, earth, and the divine are equal. It is an alternative her-story narrative that reclaims her agency along with the Nahua people in her region who because of their race, sex, class and skin color were systematically denied a voice.

74. Arenal and Powell, *Answer*, 65.

75. Sayers Peden, *Sor Juana Inés de la Cruz*, 124, 126.

76. Zimmerman, *Dictionary of Classical Mythology*, 285.

77. León-Portilla, *Aztec Thought and Culture*, 61.

78. Sayers Peden, *Sor Juana Inés de la Cruz*, 129.

For Sor Juana, this alternative world and society was in striking contrast to the one in which she lived, which was noisy, which is to say, patriarchal, characterized by terror and suspicion. For her, silence was harmony in this universe while noise, or patriarchy, inhibited it. For her, if the God of silence reigned then all the people in her region, Spaniards and non-Spaniards, would be liberated from oppressive forces deemed *imago dei*, made in God's image and likeness. In this world, individuals would be free to live out their respective belief systems and traditions. Her worldview was rooted in a Nahua ethics and Mesoamerican thought where God was manifest in unity, equilibrium, harmony, and silence. For Sor Juana, it did not matter whether your g/God was one or many. In fact, her *sueño* was panentheistic; meaning that her understanding of the world was that God permeated all of creation. Sor Juana's *sueño* was an invitation for all people to foster non-patriarchal attitudes and ideologies that inhibited interrelatedness of all people with the cosmos. Her *sueño* shared qualities valued by feminists, ecofeminists, and Latina theologians in the North and South. In this meta-narrative, the goddess Diana and the mythical character, Harpocrates, "the god of silence," would lead humanity toward the fulfillment of her *sueño*. In this world, God's beauty was manifest in all creation. In this world:

> [T]he humble shepherd and the royal prince, marking no difference between the silk of kings and peasant's woolen stuff, for slumber's trickle, in its omnipotence, grants no favor to any living being, from Pope whose sovereign tiara is from three golden circlets cast to lowly rustic in his hut of thatch, from the Emperor in his Danube palace to laborer beneath a roof of reeds, as, with undiscriminating rule.[79]

79. Ibid.

CHAPTER 6

A Paradigm for a Latina
Liberative Ecclesiology

Introduction

THE AIMS OF THIS book were two-fold: First, to examine Sor Juana Inés de la Cruz's life and texts through a gender specific lens paying attention to gaps that exist in her biographical account; and second, to examine the intersection of Sor Juana's life and texts with her subsequent censure of patriarchally-based inequalities in seventeenth-century New Spain.

For this study, I used the methodologies of foremost Catholic feminist theologians Elisabeth Schüssler Fiorenza and Rosemary Radford Ruether. Schüssler Fiorenza's methodology is a feminist historical reconstruction, while Radford Ruether's is a feminist liberationist and ecological approach. In this her-story project of Sor Juana Inés de la Cruz's life and texts, both methodologies provided the heuristic lens to understand the oppressive social and sexual codes for women in New Spain. They also helped me to understand the origins of Sor Juana's lifelong project and its suppression by later clerics.

Schüssler Fiorenza's methodology heightened my awareness that Sor Juana moved through three communities of women. As a girl, Sor Juana grew up surrounded by six women, including her mother, grandmother, full and step-sisters. As a young adult, Sor Juana was deeply influenced by the patronage of multiple *virreinas* situated in New Spain's viceregal court, in Mexico City. As a mature adult, Sor Juana lived in a community of religious women in the convent of Santa Paula, for more than twenty-five years. I argue that these communities of women were formative in molding Sor Juana's assessment of the widespread inequalities in New Spain. This hypothesis is confirmed in Octavio Paz's assertion that Sor Juana's critiques of sexism were "a visceral reflection rooted in personal lived experiences."[1]

In Sor Juana's life her two full sisters, Josefa and María, and possibly her mother, were abandoned by their husbands, or partners.[2] In response, Sor Juana secured a loan for her older sister Josefa, while in the convent, so that she could provide for herself and her four children.[3] Similarly, Sor Juana helped her elder sister María by caring for her abandoned daughter, Isabel Ramírez, in the convent of Santa Paula.[4] While there, this same niece, now her protégée Sister Isabel María de San José, was threatened by a nephew who tried to appropriate her assets.[5] In this situation, Sor Juana advocated on her behalf, preventing this injustice from happening. For a period of time as well, Sor Juana sheltered her two step-sisters, Inés and Antonia, in the convent of Santa Paula, possibly to protect their virtue before they married.[6] In the final years of Sor Juana's life, she intentionally consolidated all of her financial assets into a single account to cover the costs of daily living for her niece, upon her death. In light of these factors what I have learned about Sor Juana's Inés de la Cruz is that like her mother Doña Isabel Ramírez, she was an enterprising, spirited woman, as Paz asserts.[7] She and her mother were also important matriarchs in the larger Ramírez de Santillana familial kinship network. I suspect both Doña Isabel Ramírez and Sor Juana held the family together.

1. Paz, *Sor Juana*, 68.
2. Ibid., 66–67.
3. Ibid., 67.
4. Ibid., 68.
5. Ibid., 69.
6. Ibid., 76.
7. Ibid., 67.

Radford Ruether's methodology aided me in testing the hypothesis that Sor Juana was not only an early feminist for her time but also an ecofeminist. Her methodology helped me evaluate Sor Juana's texts for alternative interpretations of Christian scriptures, traditions and doctrines that emphasized the liberative nature of God. Her feminist lens also enabled me to see nuances in Sor Juana's sensitivity to *la tierra* (land or earth) that made up all of God's creation. This insight led me to ask the question: in what stages of Sor Juana's life did these influences emerge? My research revealed that these influences dated to the first stage of her life, living on the haciendas of Nepantla and Panoáyan, the epicenter of a once thriving Aztec capital city, Tenochtitlan. This was where Sor Juana was exposed to the ancient wisdom of the Nahua Mesoamerican population, descendants of the Aztecs.

Another insight gleaned in light of Radford Ruether's liberationist approach was that Sor Juana was more of a philosopher than a theologian. Though she engaged theological themes, Sor Juana did so within a philosophical framework where her focus was the existential question of what it meant to be human. This question emerged from testimonies and her personal experiences of seeing people treated inhumanely. Like Radford Ruether, Sor Juana was interested in varied interpretations or ideas and how they could be used as a resource for liberatory paradigms for all people and the earth. Consequently, in Sor Juana's writings one sees the mixing and blending of Mesoamerican, Christian and non-Christian ideas, ideologies, mythic figures, and culture into a Christian narrative that welcomes all. Unlike the Church, in which a singular male deity, omnipotent and transcendent, was worshipped, Sor Juana embraced a panentheistic understanding of God and the cosmos as living entities best characterized by harmony, equilibrium and balance between all people, the earth, and human and nonhuman nature.

For this feminist reconstruction of Sor Juana Inés de la Cruz's life and texts the methodologies of Schüssler Fiorenza and Radford Ruether enabled me to create a new account not only of Sor Juana's life but also a trajectory of her evolving sensitivity, in all three stages, to inequalities based on gender and race. Though three centuries separate them, Sor Juana, Schüssler Fiorenza, and Radford Ruether have developed anthropologies that advocate life and the full humanity of peoples and the earth. For they know from personal experience the devastating affects of patriarchy, sexism and violence in women's lives as a result of social structures and ideologies that are more interested in power than in the flourishing of all people. In the Roman Catholic Church, Sor Juana Inés de la Cruz's legacy has not yet been recognized. In this feminist reconstruction of Sor Juana's life and texts, my hope is that I did reclaim her legacy not only within the Christian tradition but non-Christian as well.

In fact, given her erudition and learning, Sor Juana should be named an honorary Doctor in the Roman Catholic Church. To grant Sor Juana this honor would be to recognize the on-going importance of women's resistance to a patriarchal Church hierarchy. For this to happen, however, the Church would need to share its power and authority with women, and repent of its participation in a multiplicity of oppressive ideologies and behaviors that have resulted in the dehumanization of all those who desire to live the liberating message of Jesus.

A Paradigm for a Latina Liberative Ecclesiology

What principles can be drawn from Sor Juana's life and texts for a twenty-first-century liberatory Latina ecclesiology? The values she offers are both ancient and modern.

The first is a theological anthropology based upon Sor Juana's own experiences of oppression. Like feminists today her critique of male-centered structures, ideologies, and institutions were based in personal experience. Moreover, it was this experience that laid the foundation for an alternative Christian anthropology that is liberative for all peoples and the earth. In Mesoamerican culture, the well-being of both land and humans was necessary to maintain harmony and equilibrium. Thus, we see in Sor Juana's writings her desire to perceive the land and people in a theological anthropology that values everything as beautiful, made in God's image and likeness. I suspect Sor Juana wanted to return to the time before the conquest in her region when outside forces disrupted this harmonious *paradiso, sueño*. Her anthropology affirmed the interdependence and interrelatedness of all life forms. For her, balance and harmony in the world reflected God's cosmic and human diversity.

Sor Juana also valued diverse ways of knowing. Unlike the Church that understood the world in dualistic terms, Sor Juana was grounded in the sensibilities of the Mesoamerican people that understood the world in complementary egalitarian pairs, men and women, gods and goddesses.[8] Thus, her anthropology comprised a divinely regulated world that transcended patriarchy. Though Sor Juana did not use the term "feminist," the principles underlying her argument for a more egalitarian world reflect the definition of feminism and ecofeminism given in Chapter 1.

The link in Sor Juana Inés de la Cruz's life and texts, between feminists past and present, is the intersection of her social location, lived experiences and subsequent critique of patriarchy in all its forms. She challenged both secular and religious worldviews that were used to exclude and undermine the full humanity of women and non-Spaniards of her day. Her remonstrances led her to reconsider systems of thought that undermined the full humanity of all people and creation. Her genius lay in her ability to mix and blend different ideas and worldviews in such a way that reconciliation was possible between Spanish and non-Spanish, Christians and the Nahua Mesoamerican peoples. Sor Juana's legacy is that she united her Spanish and Nahua sides in her presentation of a *sueñō/ temictli* for a more harmonious world where noise and silence are balanced. For her, both cultures had the potential to create a more just world, a model for Latina feminists today, who might walk in culturally-, socially-, or racially-mixed worlds.

8. Marcos, "Women's Religious Space in Mexico," 255.

Conclusion

Because noise and silence still reign in our twenty-first century world there is always a need for more research. More feminist historical reconstruction projects are needed. The two nameless women Sor Juana identifies in Chapter 1, who were in her litany of women religious, beg further attention. Like so many women, their lives, texts and contributions in Christian history continue to remain unknown. The starting point for this endeavor will be the pioneering book authored by Electa Arenal and Stacey Schlau who in 1989 wrote *Untold Sisters: Hispanic Women In Their Own Works*. Arenal and Schlau's book uniquely engages feminist historical reconstruction research using primary resources and archival documents.

Santa Rosa of Lima, the first *mestiza* saint beatified in the Americas, also bears further investigation. Was she, like Sor Juana, a pawn in a political game instigated by the Church and Spanish Crown? Or, did she serve a function similar to that of Our Lady of Guadalupe, bridging the divide between two distinctly different civilizations and worldviews?

I am certainly interested in a number of women María Helena Sánchez Ortega mentions in her article, "Women as Source of 'Evil' in Counter Reformation Spain." Her research shows that women in Spanish America were persecuted far more than men by the Spanish Inquisition. Who were these women? Were they *curanderas*, that is, women healers within the Nahua tradition? This research will build on the scholarship of Mesoamerican specialist, Syliva Marcos, who asserts that *curanderas* in the Nahua Mesoamerican culture held positions of authority in the community as mediums between the universe and the divine.[9] In Sor Juana's time these women were a considerable threat to both the Church and the Spanish Crown in a post- conquest world.

Lastly, on a personal level, I am interested in creating curricula based on Mesoamerican principles that values diversity among all living species, human and non-human. Like Sor Juana, I will mix and blend the teachings and philosophy of indigenous peoples

9. Ibid., 253–254.

with European values in order to create a world of balance and harmony. My *sueño* is that like Sor Juana, Roman, Greek, Nahua and Christian philosophers in the past that I too will "retrace the path from [a] civilized [humanity] who lives so far from nature," to a humanity that lives in close companionship with nature.[10] In the process, I hope in some way that, like Sor Juana and her ancestors, I will also engage in the work of transformative change: in Quechua, a *pachacuti,* or cosmic cataclysm.[11]

10. Hamilton, *Mythology,* 10, 13.
11. Gutiérrez, *We Drink From Our Own Wells,* 11.

Bibliography

Alvarado Navarrete, Elia G. *Versos A Los Versos de Sor Juana*. Mexico: Universidad Autónoma del Estado de México, 2000.

Anton, Ferdinand. *Women in Pre-Columbian America*. New York: Abner Schram, 1973.

Aquino, María Pilar and Maria José Rosado-Nunes. *Feminist Intercultural Theology: Latina Explorations for a Just World*. Maryknoll, New York: Orbis Books, 2007.

Arenal, Electa and Amanda Powell. *The Answer: La Respuesta*. New York: The Feminist Press, 2009.

Arenal, Electa and Stacey Schlau. *Untold Stories: Hispanic Nuns in Their Own Works*. Albuquerque: University of New Mexico Press, 1989.

St. Augustine's Abbey. *The Book of Saints: A Dictionary of the Servants of God*. Connecticut: Morehouse Publishing, 1989.

Bauer, Ralph and Jose Antonio Mazzotti. *Creole Subjects in the Colonial Americas*. U.S.A.: The University of North Carolina Press, 2009.

Bennett, Herman L. *Africans in Colonial Mexico: Absolutism, Christianity, and Afro-Creole Consciousness, 1570–1640*. Bloomington, IN: Indiana University Press, 2003.

Berens, E. M. *The Myths and Legends of Ancient Greece and Rome*. Road Town, Tortola, British Virgin Islands, Winchester, and Boston: Longwood Press LTD, 1979.

Bernal, Ignacio. *Tenochtitlan en una isla*. Mexico: Fondo de Cultura Económica, 1992.

Blanton, Richard, et. al. *Mesoamerica: A Comparison of Change in Three Regions*. Canada: Cambridge University Press, 1993.

Brandenburg, Doris M. "Sor Juana Inés de la Cruz: Her Life and Time." M.A.: Claremont Graduate University, 1948.

Burns, Kathryn. *Colonial Habits: Convents and the Spiritual Economy of Cuzco Peru*. Durham and London: Duke University Press, 1999.

Carrasco, Davíd. *Religions of Mesoamerica: Cosmovision and Ceremonial Centers*. Long Grove, Illinois: Waveland Press, Inc., 1990.

Castro Leal, Antonio. *Sor Juana Inés de la Cruz: Poesia, Teatro y Proso*. Mexico: Editorial Porrua, S.A., 1965.

Bibliography

Cervantes, Enríque A. *Testamento de Sor Juana Inés de la Cruz y otros documentos*. Mexico: E.A. Cervantes, 1949.

Christ, Carol P. and Judith Plaskow. *Women Spirit Rising: A Feminist Reader in Religion*. New York: Harper Collins Publishers, 1992.

Cruz, Anne J. and Mary Elizabeth Perry. *Cultural Encounters: The Impact of the Inquisition in Spain and the New World*. Berkeley: University of California Press, 1991.

De Sahagun, Fr. Bernardino. *Historía General De las Cosas de Nueva España: Tomo IV, Libro XII.=La Conquista de Mexico*. Mexico, D.F.: Editorial Pedro Robredo, 1938.

España, Guillermo. *La Familia de Sor Juana Inés de la Cruz*. Mexico City: Imprenta Universitaria, 1947.

Flynn, Gerard. *Sor Juana Inés de la Cruz*. New York: Twayne Publishers, Inc., 1971.

Franco, Jean. *Plotting Women: Gender and Representation in Mexico*. New York: Columbia University Press, 1989.

Gaspar de Alba, Alicia. *Sor Juana's Second Dream*. Albuquerque: The University of New Mexico Press, 1999.

Gebara, Ivone. *Ecofeminism in Latin America: Women From The Margins*. New York: Orbis Books, 2006.

———. *Las Aguas de Mi Pozo: Reflexiones Sobre Experiencias de Libertad*. Montevideo, Uruguay: Doble Clic, 2005.

———. *Out of the Depths: Women's Experience of Evil and Salvation*. Minneapolis: Fortress Press, 2002.

———. *El Rostro Oculto Del Mal: Una Teología Desde La Experiencia de las Mujeres*. Madrid: Editorial Trotta, 2000.

———. *Longing for Running Water: Ecofeminism and Liberation*. Minneapolis: Fortress Press, 1999.

———. "A Feminist Perspective on Enigmas and Ambiguities in Religious Interpretations." In *Popular Catholicism in a World Church: Seven Case Studies*, 256–264. New York: Orbis Books, 1999.

———. "The Trinity and Human Experience: An Ecofeminist Approach." In *Women Healing Earth: Third World Women on Ecology, Feminism, and Religion*, 13–23. New York: Orbis Books, 1996.

———. "Women Doing Theology in Latin America." In *Feminist Theology from the Third World: A Reader*, 413–425. New York: Orbis Books, 1994.

———. *Levántate y Anda: Algunos Aspectos del Caminar de la Mujer en América Latina*. Mexico: Ediciones Dabar, 1990.

Giles, Mary E. *Women in the Inquisition: Spain and the New World*. Baltimore, Maryland: The John Hopkins University, 1999.

Goizueta, Roberto. *Christ Our Companion: Toward a Theological Aesthetics of Liberation*. Maryknoll, New York: Orbis Books, 2009.

González-Andrieu, Cecilia. *Bridge to Wonder: Art as the Gospel of Beauty*. Texas: Baylor University Press, 2012.

Gonzalez, Michelle A. *Created in God's Image: An Introduction to Feminist Theological Anthropology*. Maryknoll, New York: Orbis Books, 2007.

———. *Sor Juana: Beauty and Justice in the Americas*. New York: Orbis Books, 2003.

Gomez, Ermilo Abreu. *La Ruta de Sor Juana*. Mexico: D.A.P.P., 1938.

Gutiérrez, Gustavo. *We Drink from Our Own Wells: The Spiritual Journey of a People*. Maryknoll, New York: Orbis Books, 2003.

———. *Las Casas: In Search of the Poor of Jesus Christ*. Maryknoll, New York: Orbis Books, 1995.

Hamilton, Edith. *Mythology: Timeless Tales of Gods and Heroes*. New York and Scarborough, Ontario: A Mentor Book, 1969.

Harss, Luis. *Sor Juana's Dream*. New York: Lumen Books, 1986.

Howe, George and G.A. Herrer. *A Handbook of Classical Mythology*. New York: F.S. Crofts & Co., 1929.

Isasi-Díaz, Ada María, *En la Lucha/In the Struggle: Elaborating a Mujerista Theology*. Minneapolis: Fortress Press, 2004.

———. *Mujerista Theology: A Theology for the Twenty-First Century*. Maryknoll, New York: Orbis Books, 1996.

Kidd, Beresford J. *The Counter-Reformation: 1550–1600*. London: Society for Promoting Christian Knowledge, 1933.

Kirk, Pamela. *Sor Juana Inés de la Cruz: Religion, Art, and Feminism*. New York: Continuum, 1998.

Kirk Rappaport, Pamela. *Sor Juana Inés de la Cruz: The Classics in Western Spirituality*. New York: Paulist Press, 2005.

Kramer, Heinrich and James Sprenger. *Malleus Maleficarum*. Translated by Montague Summers. USA: Digireads.com Publishing, 2009.

Lavrin, Asunción. "Sexuality in Colonial Mexico: A Church Dilemma." In *Sexuality & Marriage in Colonial Latin America*, 47–95. U.S.A.: University of Nebraska Press, 1989.

———. "Unlike Sor Juana? The Model Nun in the Religious Literature of Colonial Mexico." In *Feminist Perspectives on Sor Juana Inés de la Cruz*, 61–85. Detroit: Wayne State University Press, 1991.

Leonard, Irving A. *Times in Old Mexico: Seventeenth-Century Persons, Places and Practices*. Ann Arbor: The University of Michigan Press, 1959.

León-Portilla, Miguel. *Aztec Thought and Culture*. U.S.A: University of Oklahoma Press, 1990.

———. *The Broken Spears: The Aztec Account of the Conquest of Mexico*. Boston: Beacon Press, 1962.

Marcos, Sylvia. *Taken from the Lips: Gender and Eros in Mesoamerican Religions*. Leiden, Boston: Brill, 2006.

———. "Embodied Religious Thought: Gender and Categories in Mesoamerica." In *Gender/Bodies/Religions*, 93–99. Mexico: ALER Publications, 2000.

———. "Mesoamerican Religions." In *Encyclopedia of Women and World Religion*, 652–655. U.S.A.: Macmillan Library Reference, 1998.

Mausolff, A.J.M. *Saint Companions for each Day*. London: St. Paul Publications, 1959.

McHugh, O.P., John A. and Charles J. Callan. *Catechism of The Council of Trent For Parish Priests: Issued by Order of Pope Pius V*. Rockford, Illinois: Tan Books and Publishers, Inc., 1982.

Merrim, Stephanie. *Feminist Perspectives on Sor Juana Inés de la Cruz*. Detroit: Wayne State University Press, 1991.

Miles, Margaret R. *The Word Made Flesh: A History of Christian Thought*. Massachusetts, Oxford, and Australia: Blackwell Publishing, 2005.

Miller, Mary Ellen. *The Art of Mesoamerica: From Olmec to Aztec*. New York: Thames & Hudson, Inc., 2001.

Miller, Mary Ellen and Karl Taube. *The Gods and Symbols of Ancient Mexico and the Maya*. New York: Thames and Hudson, Inc., 1993.

Minnich, Nelson H. *Councils of the Catholic Reformation: Pisa I (1409) to Trent (1545-63)*. Great Britain and USA: Ashgate Variorum, 2008.

Mollenkott, Virginia Ramey. "Lesbian Theology." In *Dictionary of Feminist Theologies*, 166–168. Louisville, Kentucky: Westminster John Knox Press, 1996.

Morgan, Ronald J. *Spanish American Saints and the Rhetoric of Identity: 1600–1810*. Tucson, AZ: The University of Arizona Press, 2002.

Myers, Kathleen Ann. "Religious Women in Colonial Mexico." In *Encyclopedia of Women And Religion in North America*, 133–141. Bloomington and Indianapolis: Indiana University Press, 2006.

Nicholson, Irene. *Mexican and Central American Mythology*. London, New York, Sydney, and Toronto: The Hamlyn Publishing Group Limited, 1967.

Paz, Octavio. *Sor Juana or The Traps of Faith*. Cambridge: The Belknap Press of Harvard University Press, 1988.

Peters, Patricia and Renée Domeier, O.S.B. *El Divino Narciso: Sor Juana Inés de la Cruz*. Albuquerque: The University of Mexico Press, 1998.

Poma de Ayala, Felipe Guamán. *The First New Chronicle and Good Government*. U.S.A.: Hackett Publishing Company, Inc., 2006.

Radford Ruether, Rosemary. *Christianity and Social Systems: Historical Constructions and Ethical Challenges*. Lanham, Boulder, New York, Plymouth, UK: Rowman & Littlefield Publishers, Inc., 2009.

———. *Christianity and the Making of the Modern Family: Ruling Ideologies, Diverse Realities*. Boston: Beacon Press, 2000.

———. *Sexism and God-Talk: Toward a Feminist Theology*. Boston: Beacon Press, 1993.

———. *Gaia & God: An Ecofeminist Theology of Earth Healing*. New York, N.Y.: HarperCollins Publishers, 1992.

Ramírez, Guillermo. *La Familia de Sor Juana Inés de la Cruz*. Mexico: Imprenta Universitaria, 1947.

Reyes Ruiz, Jesus. *La Epoca Literaria de Sor Juana Inés de la Cruz*. Mexico: Departamento de Acción Social Universitaria, 1951.

Rivera-García, Alejandro. *The Community of the Beautiful: A Theological Aesthetics*. Collegeville, Minnesota: The Liturgical Press, 1999.

Sabat-Rivers, Georgina. "A Feminist Re-reading of Sor Juana Inés de la Cruz's Dream." In *Feminist Perspectives on Sor Juana Inés de la Cruz*, 142–169. Detroit, Michigan: Wayne State University Press, 1991.

—. *Sor Juana Inés de la Cruz: Inudación Castálida*. Madrid: Clásicos Castalia, 1982.

Salazar Mallen, Ruben. *Apuntes para una biografía de Sor Juana Inés de la Cruz*. Mexico: Editorial Stylo, 1952.

Sánchez, David A. *From Patmos to the Barrio: Subverting Imperial Myth*. Minneapolis, MN: Fortress Press, 2008.

Sánchez Ortega, María Helena. "Woman as Source of 'Evil' in Counter Reformation Spain." In *Cultural Encounters: The Impact of the Inquisition in Spain and the New World*, 196–215. Berkeley: University of California Press, 1991.

Sanders, William T. and Barbara J. Price. *Mesoamerica: The Evolution of a Civilization*. New York: Random House, 1968.

Sayers Peden, Margaret. *Sor Juana Inés de la Cruz: Poems, Protest, and a Dream*. New York: Penguin Books, 1997.

Schons, Dorothy. "Some Obscure Points in the Life of Sor Juana Inés de la Cruz." In *Feminist Perspectives on Sor Juana Inés de la Cruz*, 142–169. Detroit, Michigan: Wayne State University Press, 1991.

Schüssler Fiorenza, Elisabeth. *Bread Not Stone: The Challenge of Feminist Biblical Interpretation*. Boston: Beacon Press, 1995.

—. *In Memory of Her: A Feminist Theological Reconstruction of Christian Origins*. New York: Crossroads, 1994.

—. *But She Said: Feminist Practices of Biblical Interpretation*. Boston: Beacon Press, 1992.

—. "Discipleship of Equals." In *Dictionary of Feminist Theologies*, 70–71. Louisville, Kentucky: Westminster John Knox Press, 1996.

Schwartz, Stuart B. *Victors and Vanquished: Spanish and Nahua Views of the Conquest of Mexico*. Boston and New York: Bedford/St. Martin's, 2000.

Scott, Nina M. *Madres del Verbo: Mothers of the Word: Early Spanish American Women Writers*. Albuquerque: The University of New Mexico Press, 1999.

Silverblatt, Irene. *Modern Inquisitions: Peru and the Colonial Origins of the Civilized World*. Durham and London: Duke University Press, 2004.

Socolow, Susan Migden. *The Women of Colonial Latin America*. USA: Cambridge University Press, 2000.

Tavard, George H. *Juana Inés de la Cruz and a Theology of Beauty: The First Mexican Theology*. Notre Dame: University of Notre Dame Press, 1991.

Trueblood, Alan S. *A Sor Juana Anthology*. Cambridge, Massachusetts, and London, England: Harvard University Press, 1988.

Twinam, Ann. *Public Lives: Private Secrets, Gender, Honor, Sexuality, and Illegitimacy in Colonial Spanish America*. Stanford, California: Stanford University Press, 1999.

————. "Honor, Sexuality, and Illegitimacy in Colonial Spanish America." In *Sexuality & Marriage in Colonial Latin America*, 119–155. Lincoln and London: University of Nebraska Press, 1989.

Williams, Eloy and C. Rodriguez. *Sor Juana Inés de la Cruz: The Tenth Muse*. San Antonio, Texas: Babbit Instructional Resources, 2001.

Wissmer, Jean-Michel. "*El amigo español de Sor Juana: Talentos y ambiguidades del Padre Calleja*." In *Aproximaciones a Sor Juana*, 377–388. Mexico: FCE, 2005.

Vallejo de Villa, Augusto. "*Acerca de la loa*." In *Letras Libres*, 80–81, 118; 2001.

Vives, Juan Luis. *The Education of a Christian Woman: A Sixteenth-century Manual*. Translated by Charles Fantazzi. Chicago: Chicago University Press, 2000.

Young, Serinity. *Encyclopedia of Women and World Religion*. New York: Macmillan Reference USA, 1999.

Yugar, Theresa. "U.S. Latina Feminist Paradigm: Model of an Inclusive Twenty-first Century Ecclesiology." In *Reimagining With Christian Doctrines: Responding to Global Gender Injustices*, 90–104. New York: Palgrave Macmillan, 2014.

Lightning Source UK Ltd.
Milton Keynes UK
UKOW05f1049200317
297055UK00001B/252/P

9 781625 644404